LINES:

STORIES
and
SKETCHES

Donna Vander Griend

Lines: Stories and Sketches

First printed edition © 2024 Donna Vander Griend

To request permission, contact the publisher at
publishing@villagebooks.com

Scripture taken from *THE MESSAGE*. Copyright 1993, 1994, 1996, 2000, 2001, 2002.
Used by permission of NavPress Publishing Group.

Quotation from Father Zosima is taken from *Kiss the Earth When You Pray: The Father Zosima
Poems*, copyright 2016 by Robert Hudson, published by the Apocryphile Press.
Used with permission.

ISBN 979-8-218-37539-3

Library of Congress Control Number: 2024903064

Designed by Jill Flores
Author photo by Amy Brandt

Printed by Village Books
1200 11th Street
Bellingham, WA 98225

Visit Donna Vander Griend at donnavdg@gmail.com

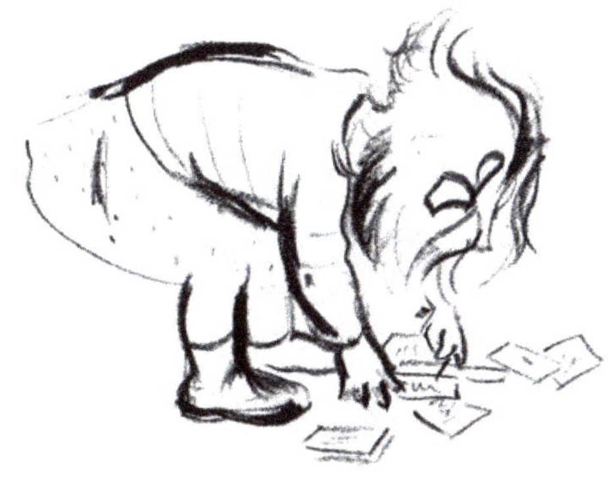

LINES speak

as we shape them into **stories** and **sketches**.

This book is hold-in-your-hands encouragement to

write your thoughts and **draw** your insights.

There is white space on every other page just for you.

Pick up a pen or pencil. Maybe add color.

Scrawl and scribble and smile.

Between you and me and God and the rest of us

the lines of creativity wait to come alive.

CONTENTS

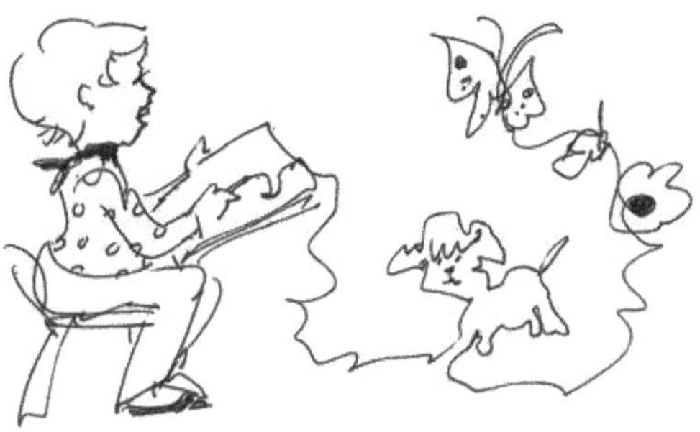

INTRODUCTORY LINES

Even though cave drawings without words predated journals without drawings, they did get together at some point in history. One might argue that a picture is worth a thousand words, or that one word can evoke a thousand scenes…but when sketch lines and story lines are on the same page, communication is more than doubly enhanced.

Every time I see a journal with inked sketches and watercolors on its pages, the images draw me to the words and the words bring me back to the images. It all started with my discovery of Edith Holden's *The Country Diary of an Edwardian Lady* published around 1906. Daily she painted birds and flowers and butterflies, captioned them with poems from the likes of Shakespeare or Robert Browning, and added her handwritten comments: "The birds have become wonderfully bold this last week since their usual hunting grounds have been buried in snow." Factual she was, and pristine.

More recently I found Danny Gregory and his book-journal called *Everyday Matters: a memoir*. He has a different perspective on birds than Edith from the Edwardian age. After sketching pigeons, he writes: "Pigeons are quite beautiful but also somehow repulsive. Maybe it's their obsession with food or their parboiled feet, the homeless of the animal world." Authentically raw and creatively graphic. His book is the imperfect, realistic story of how drawing helped him be a faithful husband to his disabled wife. Dear Edith from the last century would have been dismayed at the daring of baring one's soul.

But my most favorite sketches have come to me from a good friend and neighbor. She has no doubt spent the 10,000 hours Malcolm Gladwell, in his book *Outliers*, insists it takes to master a skill. She thinks I have done that with the writing craft. Perhaps together we could be that writer/illustrator combo dream. I would write the story of how she sketched a group of women sitting at a bus stop for a "blind contour" drawing exercise. (One of the ways artists learn to observe keenly is to focus on their subject without looking at their paper or pencil movements.) Out of concentrated blindness came a bunch of frumpled beauties, capturing delight and reality simultaneously. She touched them up later with splashes of watercolor and mass-produced them into greeting cards.

I send one to a friend who needs encouragement with a handwritten note: "This could be you, you know…a graciously aging woman with an attitude, all feisty and ready to take on the world with wide-eyed anticipation. So far we are still delighting in life and defying death…and we have each other for the journey."

In some way, we are all a bit blind as we do life. "*Seeing through a glass darkly*" was how the good ole' Apostle Paul put it. But God lets us capture beauty anyway through sketches and stories, paints and pens, cave drawings and journals. Sketch lines and story lines, a recipe for rejoicing! You, dear reader, are invited to fill every white and waiting page in this book with your own sketch lines and story lines, add a little color here and there…and let the sharing begin!

Sketch and write your own lines ⟶

LINES WRITTEN AND SKETCHED

I used to think "inspired" was synonymous with "instant."

Like Michelangelo knowing instantly that David was in that block of rock. Or Van Gogh plopping his yellow paint-filled brush on a canvas and *Voila*! Sunflowers. I could imagine a concert pianist awaiting the magic flow of electricity through her nimble fingers to make the music come alive.

Which excused any effort on my part. I would rather procrastinate and wait for that inspirational moment. I even developed a theology of heaven that claimed there would be no need to practice there. I wouldn't have to do scales interminably before I could play Beethoven. I would be able to dab just the right mix of color with the right brush with the exact amount of water to instantly produce a dazzling watercolor. I could write as if my pen had a mind of its own or my computer had a creativity button. But over the years it became clear that I was not one of the chosen for the lightning strike, if indeed anyone ever is, adding more proof to Thomas Edison's "Genius is 1% inspiration and 99% perspiration."

Lately I have had this yen to write a journal with watercolor illustrations. I have studied the prototypes on-line and immersed myself in a hand-held published one: Susan Branch's *A Fine Romance: Falling in Love with the English Countryside*. Along with her hand-written travel narrative, she sketches and water-colors red phone booths and green hedgerows and yellow lemon butter cookies into the margins. She starts her paragraphs with elegant capital letters like they do in Celtic Bibles. She quietly enhances the pages with thin brush lines or dots or dashes for borders. She makes it look so easy…

Until I buy my own little school box of watercolors. I cannot produce five little consistent dots in a row, much less make a cookie look like a cookie. Is there really no instant inspiration and production? I go online for tutorials and find thousands (everyone out there is practicing, learning tips and techniques and trying to perfect them). One woman showed at least ninety-nine ways to paint an ocean wave. And I can't even do dots.

Learn to sketch first, I conclude. I collar an artist friend of mine, hand her a sketchbook and pen, and ask her to show me how she does those "quick sketches." I thought she would start simply, like drawing a rock or a tree. She just says, *Stand there*. Then in thirty seconds she spontaneously puts my image on a page. With confidence, I might add. I am enthralled. I have yet to muster the courage to try. It was obvious she had brought fifty years of plodding practice into that spontaneous moment. I don't have that much time left. I guess I will have to wait for heaven….

For now, I am on the appreciation edge of understanding how difficult it is to imitate her gift and awestruck by what she can do, and I cannot. It could be that in a timeless heaven we can trade our gifts with one another or pursue every gift that might now be latent in our souls. Perhaps "inspired" and "instant" are somehow synonymous there. Until then, as she draws lines and I write them, may we delight in our differences! And maybe even collaborate…

Sketch and write your own lines

LINES IN THE SAND

A few generations ago we had a stereotyped version of fatherhood labeled Dictator Dad. That kind of parent would gruffly say things like, "I am drawing a line in the sand, son. And if your hairy big toe gets even close to crossing over it, I'll never let you forget it!"

On my beach-walk today, I look for lines in the sand, not left by the heavy finger or stick of a punitive father but drawn the way our Father-God has left His mark since the beginning of time. His rhythmical waves draw and erase, draw and erase. The ever-moving water leaves temporary lines for the few hours between tide changes as it slowly inches over the curve of the planet, and then gets imperceptibly brought back by some mysterious magnetism connected to the moon. And while that is happening, the Artist tilts His earth palette ever-so-slightly as He keeps on sketching in the sand…

The lines He draws are between wet and dry, between absorption and evaporation. He leaves a damp tan line down the white dry sand like T-shirt marks on the arms of a mid-western farmer. Sometimes He adds seaweed or flotsam, driftwood and broken shells, to embellish the lines.

This morning the clean, white sand canvas receives pure lines, without cumber. Wave after wave sketches lines of hilly landscapes, as if God wants the beachy edges of a continent to remember that there is beauty inland as well. The waves make their marks. Gallery titles might be "Foothills of the Rockies" or "Kentucky Blue Mountains." I spot those "Galilean Hills" where Jesus walked and preached and fed thousands, sensing Him depositing a visual for me to feel His story and His presence. Peace is afoot.

"Peace I bring you," Jesus says. He doesn't draw lines in the sand accompanied by threats like a parent who demands control. Nor does He act like us humans, so often angry, storming beaches against enemy lines to win wars. His peace is inspired by beauty and forgiveness. If only before rebellions began, we would-be enemies could walk those beaches together, reveling in the way God leaves His artistry all over this gorgeous globe, sharing His invitation of forgiveness wherever ugliness exists.

At a church service we attended, the pastor challenged us to go to one of the forty sandboxes placed around the sanctuary and write in the sand what was keeping us from fully living the way God intended. After printing out our one-word confessions, he instructed us to wipe the sand smooth for the next person. It felt like a working metaphor for finding peace with God.

John F. Gardner has said, "Life is the art of drawing without an eraser." We make a lot of mistakes that agitate us and cannot be corrected. Getting it right the very first time is too much for us. When we depend on our own feet for direction, our big toes tend to take us into threatening territory. But the ebb and flow, the washing and removing, are the un-mistakable gifts from a Fatherly hand whose eraser is forgiveness and whose art is peace.

Sketch and write your own lines

STORY LINES

I have not been able to let this "line thing" go yet.

I headed north toward threatening charcoal-colored clouds and a murky ocean that obediently reflected all that darkness. The wind was gusty. Sporadic raindrops spit-fired against my skin like so many miniscule darts finding their target. There were no smooth lines in the sand from gentle waves pushing tiny fragments of shells into place to form sketches on the beach. Far from reminding me of a quiet art gallery, there was chaos and dishevelment everywhere.

The weather outside began intruding on the weather in my heart. I became cynical. That is when my questions started bombarding the sky: Why do we keep up the struggle? What is my purpose in the universe anyway? Who even notices? Why bother?

I thought about the e-mails I had read before going on this walk. They were from friends who had worked through considerable and complex hurts, added their breakthrough stories, and thanked me for my prayers. Cynicism spoke up, saying I had nothing to do with those transformations. Other people had interacted with and prayed on behalf of these friends; they had not needed me. Each story could have moved forward without my peripheral involvement or pathetic prayers.

When the lovely sketch lines on a calm beach have disappeared, replaced with the messy debris of a storm, God comes through with something else: *Story lines.* Imagine the main characters and plots the Author brought into the Bible story. Thousands…and each one necessary to the narrative. Writer Bob Goff mentions Justus, whom none of us remember… the guy who did not win the lottery pick to be the replacement disciple for Judas Iscariot. Goff reminds us that Justus was highly qualified (or he would not have been a candidate) and most likely went on to do incredible, unsung things with his life. Justus…"just us." Goff's play on words reminds us of our common non-superhero status. But we are part of the story, no matter how little media attention we get.

If while reading a book from cover to cover we would find unfinished sentences, gaps in the middle of paragraphs, words missing, and thoughts incomplete…we would be outraged, or at the very least, crabby. *I cannot follow the story line*, we would complain. *This does not make any sense*!

We show up in someone else's story because God wrote us in. Perhaps He asks us to pray for another person, not because He gets writer's block without us, but because He wants us to have skin in the story, an investment in someone else's life. Our prayers keep us curious about the endings, making us glad for the e-mails that tell us that God has been at work and that He put us in the story line for His reasons, novel every time. Inclusion in a story, our own or another's, inevitably gives us purpose.

Our prayers for you are always spilling over into thanksgivings… We keep getting reports on your steady faith in Christ, our Jesus, and the love you continuously extend to all Christians. The **lines** *of purpose in your lives never grow slack, tightly tied as they are to your future in* **heaven**, *kept* **taut** *by hope.* — *Colossians 1:3-5*

Picture each prayer strung along that line of hope all the way to the Author's writing space. He may just use that line beaded with your love to inspire a redemptive twist in someone's story.

"*May the eyes of your heart be enlightened,*" the Apostle Paul prays. I have prayed that request for others, too. On today's walk, though, it becomes my own prayer. The strong wind is like a cleaning agent against my face and limbs, an air of freedom as it blows through my hair. Cleansing and freedom…no wonder the wind is a metaphor for the Spirit. The eyes of my heart light up with insight. I feel the sun on my back even as I walk into dark clouds, a warming that relaxes my stiffened muscles. I imagine God saying, "*I've got your back…there's nothing to fear.*" What a great line to include in this recent moment of my story!

Story lines. Who but God could create the characters and intermingle the life stories of so many?

Sketch and write your own lines ⟶

ALIGNMENT

Obviously, a creative power beyond myself is in charge of aligning the stars in their constellations and the planets in their orbits. But my certainty wobbles a bit about alignments in my own life. These days of confusions and divisions, of too many good-byes, separations, and isolations, of burden-bearing and prayer-pleading, often make me feel out of alignment with culture, church, and government, with what God ultimately has in mind for us humans.

But then, almost daily, my soul re-aligns with truth, spoken and written. God manages to open the eyes of my heart and the thoughts of my brain to understand. Sometimes it is the simplicity of reading a verse from the Bible that clarifies once again, or comforts. This morning it was Jesus's words: "…*my peace I give to you; not as the world gives do I give to you. Let not your hearts be troubled, neither let them be afraid.*" — *John 14:27*

God also arranges experiences just for me, both mundane and extraordinary. Mysteriously He aligns innumerable things into an event that megaphones this truth: *I am. And I am here!*

Last Tuesday an alignment adventure awaited. Time had to align with geography which had to align with circumstance that placed me with a friend in a small town on an island invited to a dinner party. Not feeling inclined to go, I entered this awkward situation with my not-up-to-par elderly self, a misfit in a group of talented artists, wanting to be a blessing rather than a burden, but instead, focused on where to sit to alleviate arthritic pain.

And then she sits next to me. A young Mexican artist who had come all the way from Chile to take this particular painting course on this island off Washington state's coastline. How many alignments did it take to meet at this moment in this place smack-dab in the present? Just a Tuesday picnic in this twenty-first century and we both "just happened" to be there.

In broken English she began sharing her story. I heard of her roots and her family, her marriage, and accomplishments (all those planned alignments on her way). I learned that during this recent trip she had been able to visit the church in southern Mexico where her art pieces, featuring the Stations of the Cross on stone, were newly hung on the white plastered walls. She explained her artistic process to me, a year-long emotional immersion of walking with and understanding Jesus. "How do you say in English?" She tries to tell me how she "scratched" off the surface of each stone and "was given" the painting method to make stone look translucent with Light.

And yes, she had photos of her art on her phone. She extended her handheld face of Christ to me. I saw …and burst into joyous tears. And then, so did she.

An alignment of wonder. Our souls felt a one-ness. Together we recognized the "*I am here*" presence of a crucified but risen Christ. I have never responded in spontaneous tears to a painting until this moment, this alignment-of-now. She hugged me long with the gratefulness of an artist whose work had worked deeply in another. We both reveled in this surprise of joy, knowing that together we had been moved by the God of the universe into an alignment of the best kind.

Sketch and write your own lines

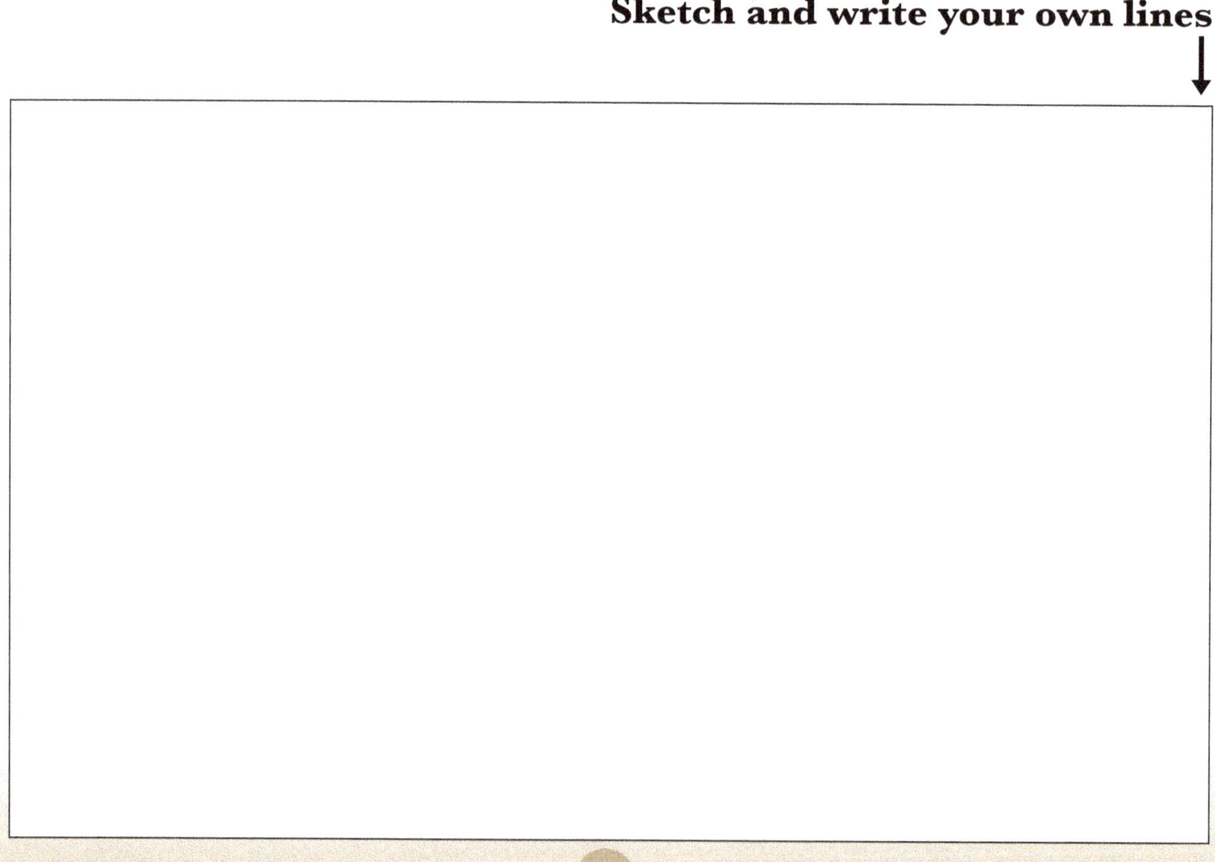

STICK PEOPLE

"Baw with me, Grandma," toddler Malakai invites as he walks into our kitchen after being dropped off for some grandma-care with his brother Josiah. I start translating: "Ball? Do you want to play with the ball, Malakai?"

"No," he says. "Baw."

Maybe he's hungry. "Bread? Do you want a piece of bread?"

He impatiently shakes his little head, "No. Baw!" I extract his pesky pacifier to give him more consonant possibilities.

"What do you want, Malakai?" "Baw," he repeats dejectedly, even with his lips free. The helplessness of not communicating with my grandson shrouds my soul in sadness. We are stuck, two entities with no entry into the other's meaning.

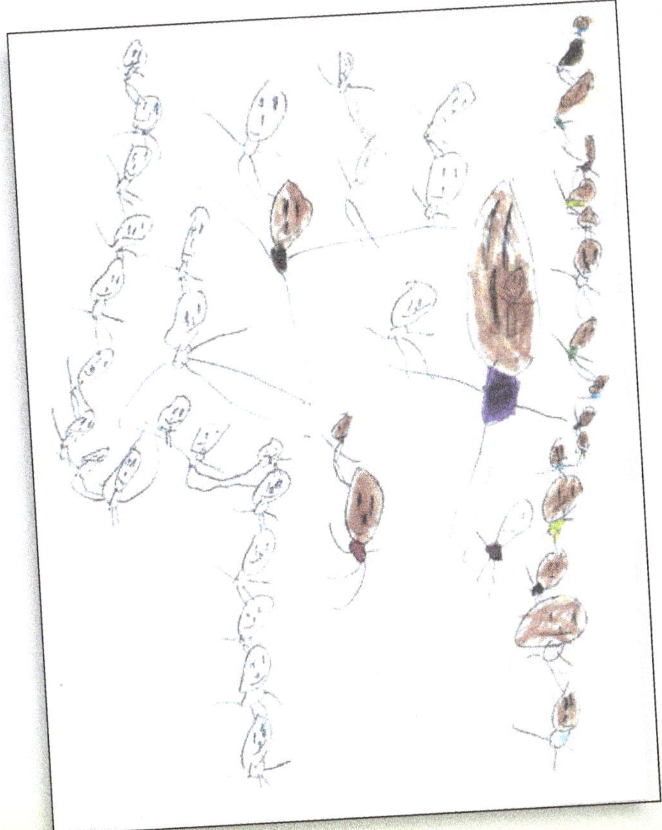

"Josiah, what does *Baw* mean? What is your brother trying to tell me?" I plead with my five-year-old interpreter.

"He wants to *draw*, Grandma," he easily explains.

I sigh at our breakthrough. Malakai smiles broadly and scooches into place by the table while I gather art supplies for the three of us. He *baws* with uninhibited delight, thickly smearing large blobs of color with brush, fingers, hands and elbows.

Josiah shows his artistic flair by choosing a pencil and speedily filling his paper with stick men. He makes a circle head, an oval body, and four spider-wispy lines for arms and legs. In no time he completely fills his paper with not less than forty figures, his version of a paper universe filled with people. He doesn't stop there. He pulls another unblemished white page in front of him and says, "Grandma, get your own pencil. You can do this with me." I comply and listen to further instruction.

"We'll take turns," he says. "I'll go first." Another instant-art person lands on the page. "Now you draw someone, Grandma."

This looks easy. I am attaching the second leg line, when Josiah begins correcting me. "Not that way, Grandma," he says. His teacher side comes through: "Every guy has to touch another guy." I recouped myself from being in the wrong by eyeing his first masterpiece lying on the table beside us. Sure enough, every limb on the page is anchored to a head or body or another limb, forty stick people stuck to each other.

His message is community. Together we fill this page with another village full of skinny natives. He colors in the "clothing" and bodies of our Adam and Eve descendants. When he finishes, I know without a doubt that the natives have brought in people from other races and nations. The page is full of people of color, people who need each other to survive, people who can only fill out their wispiness as they love one another.

Over the ensuing weeks, Josiah draws pages and pages of "people in community," daily putting pencil-to-paper to pursue his theme. I confiscate his art stationery and send it to someone who may need to know there's another stick person out there who cares. As I write and mail, I hear the echoes of a preschool rabbi still interpreting for me:

"Everybody has to touch another person, Grandma."

Thank-you Creator God that you are not disappointed with these wispy lines that define us. Day by day your love fills the hearts of the crooked sticks that we are. We give you our full-bodied praise. Amen

Sketch and write your own lines ⟶

BOTTOM LINES

When remodeling a basement or buying a car, the foremost question is, "How much?" But it is not culturally acceptable to begin there. The contractor talks about "if this, then that" and waffles about the estimate. The used car salesperson negotiates, lowers and adds, talks to the manager, lowers and adds some more until the buyer, clearly restraining built-up frustration, finally asks, "But what's the bottom line?"

Even more difficult is sorting out one's values and beliefs by wisely discerning truth. Is there a way to know truth's bottom-line conclusion without having to listen to and filter out a long, convoluted discussion? And what about the "much reading of books?" There are words, words, words everywhere that require my listening or understanding, but to whom and for what? My lazy-default goal is to quickly know the bottom line so that I can either 'be right' or 'get it right.' My desire for shortcuts goes back to my early years, ever since my father assumed the role of tutor when I was in my teens, letting me struggle to "get" a geometry problem. I was convinced that wasting time and effort, plus the wearing down of patience, could have been avoided had he just given me the answer.

We could simply change this subject without changing the words. Consider Bottom's lines. Bottom was a comedic character in Shakespeare's play *Midsummer Night's Dream* who came off as a funny guy because he was blissfully unaware of his own ridiculousness. Bottom's foolishness comes to a head when his own head turns into that of an ass. The lovely Titania has been doused with a potion that causes her to fall in love with the first person she sees upon awakening. It is Bottom…the ass. And here is that famous Bottom line spoken to Titania as she swoons over him:

> *Methinks, mistress, you should have little reason*
> *for that [swooning]: and yet, to say the truth, reason and*
> *love keep little company together now-a-days.*

Love does not always make sense and bottom lines are not always conclusive no matter who says them.

Though their writing is sometimes obfuscated and veiled, most novelists want their readers to know the key message of a book they have been working on for years. During the pandemic, I read a novel about a Russian aristocrat who was in exile for decades, sheltered-in-place in a one hundred square foot apartment on the sixth floor of an old hotel. It took until page 418 in *A Gentleman in Moscow* before author Amor Towles clearly stated his bottom line: "Showing a sense of personal restraint that was almost out of character, the Count had restricted himself to two succinct pieces of parental advice. The first was that if one did not master one's circumstances, one was bound to be mastered by them; and the second was Montaigne's maxim that the surest sign of wisdom is constant cheerfulness." There now.

A friend-couple of ours recently began persuasion arguments to encourage us to buy a place in Arizona for wintering. She writes: *Bottom line: you'd have activities to enjoy, people to meet and friendships to forge.* The phrase *Bottom line* filled me with the refreshing clarity that capsulizes truth and motivates action. But we did not buy the property…

All of us have heard innumerable bottom lines in our lifetimes. They run the gamut from ridiculous to profound:

- The **bottom line** to potty training is that every child will eventually be potty trained.
- Whether you are looking for a mixer or cappuccino maker, the **bottom line** is that you want an appliance that works.
- They will probably not reveal the **bottom line** amount to you in the hopes that they can get you to settle for an amount higher than that.
- The bottom line is, there is no **bottom line** — or at least it's very unlikely.

A final statement about bottom lines: Keep listening and searching for them. Embrace the serious ones and the seriously crazy ones. Ponder them or preach them. Enjoy their pivotal points with laughter. Borrow or invent them. Reaching any conclusion is a zigzag of a process; a bottom line is your easy-to-remember shortcut.

Here is "the conclusion of the matter" from an epic piece of poetry entitled *Ecclesiastes*. The king-poet Solomon writes long and hard about life's disappointments, but toward the end, he bottom-lines his thoughts with an encouraging call-for-action:

The last and final word is this:
Fear God.
Do what he tells you.
And that's it.
— Ecclesiastes 12:13

A LINE OF QUESTIONING

You [God] asked, "Who is this muddying the water,
ignorantly confusing the issue,
second-guessing my purposes?"

— *Job 42:3a*

Sam and Jack are ready to go home. They settle into the backseat of the van. Changing from 'reverse' to 'drive' gear, I remember several things I have forgotten. I cut the motor and promise my grandsons a quick return. Re-entering the house, I gather the coffee thermos, a rain jacket, the book their mother wanted to borrow, and check whether I had turned off the laminating machine. Minutes later I am back in the driver's seat.

"What did you talk about while I was gone?" I ask, eyeing them in the rearview mirror as we make our way down the driveway.

"Nothing," Sam answers. "We just sat in 'companionable silence.'" I smile at this vocabulary nugget my 4th grader has pulled from the stream of words he prospects every time he listens or reads.

"Great phrase, Sam. Where did it come from?" the English teacher in me asks.

"It appears at least once in about every book I read," he answers with the airs of the well-read.

Companionable little brother Jack breaks his half of the silence: "Sam's reading sometimes bugs me cuz he does it so much when I just want to play with him." He pauses and then, with second grade wisdom, says, "But I guess he's learning things from books."

"Where else do you learn things?" I ask.

"From the web," they agree in unison.

"Do you think there are answers for every single question you could ever think of?" I toss out from the front seat, reflecting my impatience with those who believe that searching the internet produces undeniable truth.

"Probably not," Sam says. "Like, 'Does your image stay in the mirror after you walk away?' or 'Does a falling tree make a noise in the forest if no one is near to hear it?' Are there answers for those?"

Neither of us answers.

Then Jack says, "Sometimes Sam gives me an answer I don't understand."

"Yeah. I'm vague in my answers," Sam smirks as if that is a good thing.

My mind crafts questions as we drive along in more 'companionable silence':

If an answer is vague and hard to understand, is it really an answer? Is our endless searching simply a spawning ground for more questions? Will we ever be satisfied? Was Socrates right when he insisted that asking questions was the best teaching method?

I think of Job who had more questions than most of us and whose friends, unasked, gave a book-full of advice and answers. Toward the end of that book, when God asks Job a question, *"Who is this muddying the water…?"* Job says, "I admit it. I was the one. I babbled on about things far beyond me, made small talk about wonders way over my head."

Then God says, "Listen, and let me do the talking. Let me ask the questions:

"Where were you when I created the earth?" — Job 38:4

"Have you ever gotten to the true bottom of things?" — Job 38:1

"So to whom will you compare me, the Incomparable?" — Isaiah 46:5a

"Can you picture me without reducing me?" — Isaiah 46:5b

Unanswerable questions, all. They teach us who we really are: vague babblers in a continual state of grappling. They teach us who we are not: God. Humbled, we hear God ask each of us the most pivotal question of all: "Who do you say that I am?"

Sketch and write your own lines ⟶

BOUNDARY LINES

We tell the visitors and vacationers who choose to wander through our wilderness in Montana that they cannot get lost. A hundred-acre-wood and a lake owned by loons, its boundary lines are clear: a fence line, a somewhat meandering river, and a country road. Eventually they stumble on to one of these three existing landmarks, follow it, and find their way 'home' to the cabin compound.

Boundaries are helpful. I think of my mother teaching me how to embroider when I was a mere six years old. Setting the hoop to stretch the fabric was task #1 before the creativity and colorful stitching could begin. Having that framework in place made the difference between sloppy and lovely.

Years ago, there was a New York Times bestseller called *Boundaries* that is still being updated. Drs. Henry Cloud and John Townsend taught avid readers when to say "yes" and how to say "no," setting healthy boundaries with their spouse, children, friends, parents, co-workers, and even with themselves. Perhaps it was timely to become aware of how we step out-of-bounds in our relationships, but we watched with some concern as people began drawing protective lines around themselves fed by our cultural propensity for individualism and avoidance.

Before all the how-to books, God gave the ten commandments, boundaries that have helped us live in community for centuries (keep sabbaths, honor parents, no murder, adultery, stealing, lying, lusting, envy, cursing…and no idols). He also gave each of us our very own conscience, a created-within moral compass that points or guides or warns, sometimes with a gut reaction to the red flags messing with our insides. Which brings to mind another bestseller in the psychosomatic field: *The Body Keeps the Score* by Bessel Van Der Kolk, M.D. Boundaries, it seems, can be laid by fences, books, commandments, a conscience, or guts.

I love the love story from 2020 that happened when the the US-Canadian border was closed during the pandemic. The wedding date had been set long before, but the bride was from the U.S. and the groom from Canada and neither of them could legally cross the boundary between their two countries. So, from both sides of the border they gathered the preacher and their attendants and their families and themselves, then met at the ditch that separates Washington State from British Columbia, shouted their vows and congratulations to one another, and trusted the promise that someday they would no longer be apart. Bridges can be built over boundaries…

Land borders and emotional boundaries are necessary…for keeping the peace. But generating peace also means breaching barriers to reach out and extend love to others. Unlike the lethargy that isolation causes, we are filled with an energy that intimacy generates when we are physically and personally present to each other. Often, we would do well to cross relational barriers and gave each other a hug.

A friend asked that her favorite verse, Psalm 16:6, be in her obituary as a thank you note to God:

> *LORD…the boundary lines have fallen for me in pleasant places;*
> *surely I have a delightful inheritance. — NIV*

There is one last, inevitable boundary we will all cross…that line between death and life.

After that, separations will be forever non-existent. We will be with a God whose reach is limitless, whose forgiveness is unfathomable, whose love is unconditional, and whose eternity is without end. Essentially…a God without boundaries. People without barriers. A place without borders.

Sketch and write your own lines

BYE LINES

Saying Good-Bye. My heart feels tear-salty with sadness for a long time before the words are spoken. Then summer ends and, hopelessly hesitant, this grandmother bids September farewells to six grandchildren: one off to college, one to a year-long ballet training, two to 'seek their fortunes' in L.A., one off to France, and another back to Canada.

I felt a liquid slippage behind the back of my life as if love was trying to sneak away without my knowing. How does a grandma stop this oceanic movement of the future in the lives of those younger ones she loves so deeply? She cannot.

But in the 'summer of my discontent,' I was given these insights, heart-sights really, to comfort me, to help me turn around, look into their eyes, and send them on. First, I found myself rereading John 10 about Jesus, with His good shepherd reputation, leaving the 99 in the sheep pen while going after #100, the lost one. I had always thought that all of us, especially those we care about, need to be in that pen together in order to be safe. Apparently not so.

Moving on in His parable-telling, Jesus gets metaphoric and says, *"I am the gate."* I scrawl additions to myself: *Jesus is the pivotal person hinging all of history together, hinging my life together. Jesus can open up a life! I can swing on that gate with freedom and spontaneity, because, whether open or shut, He is grounded and strong and still holding.* I remember the birth days with joy, the 'comings,' of my precious grandchildren…I also want to trust their 'goings,' communicating to them: *Hang on and swing a little. Feel free to come and go. Jesus can lead you out and bring you back in.*

Another God-thought: *This is how I am letting you know My Presence. You will have many "didn't-see-that-coming" moments that communicate the wide embrace of my love for you and your grandchildren.* The next afternoon I met a younger woman who skipped the shallows of conversation and went at once to a deep place of vulnerability, drawing me into soulmate territory, that connection that has been called love at first sight. The way God loves. When it was time to say good-bye, she thanked me for my sensitivity and gave me a lingering hug while whispering in my ear like a wave rising behind my back, "The ocean is in your eyes."

And I learned from a newly published novel. *Sugar Birds* by Cheryl Grey Bostrom taught me how baby birds learn survival skills from their parents, but once they leave the nest, they rarely come back. The Bible says, *Consider the sparrows* and how the Heavenly Father takes care of them, *though they know it not…*

The next day I opened Instagram and found a photo of mama Maluhia saying her good-bye lines to my granddaughter. The caption reads: Fly, birdie, fly.

Jesus (who doesn't say good-byes) signs off with His by-lines, holy autographs for our stories He has breathed life into and promises to be part of…always.

I am the Good Shepherd   *I am the Gate*
I am the Bread of Life   *I am the Vine*
I am the Light of the World   *I am the Way, the Truth, and the Life*
I am the Resurrection and the Life

Sketch and write your own lines

DEADLINES

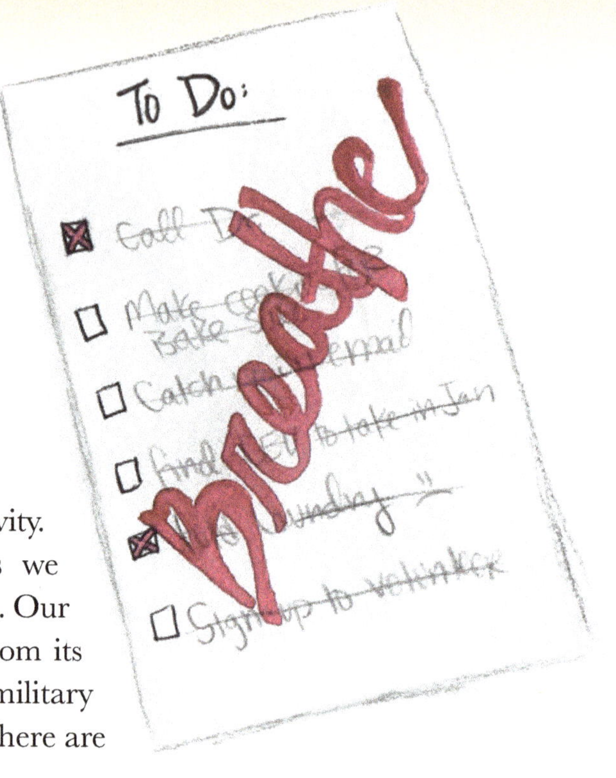

We all have deadlines to meet. Assignments to fulfill that are often motivating and full of decent work. Why then, do we use the word "dead" to describe the finish line? Completions should call for celebrations. Ahh, but there is always another deadline…

We are part of a society that worships productivity. *More* and *faster* guarantee a growing panic as we progress through our days to make those deadlines. Our achievement-oriented culture coined the word from its original meaning. Deadline: "the line around a military prison beyond which a prisoner could be shot." There are consequences should you fail. Some of them dire.

In a sense, once given a deadline, we are imprisoned until we can somehow escape. Sure, there have been less traumatic situations than being under siege, but they all carry a heaviness, a hovering that will not go away, like the security guard in the tower with a gun: March! Keep moving. A curfew looms. There is a target date, you know, a cutoff point. The term paper is due. So are your taxes. Time to deliver. Last warning. Projects. Permits. Proposals. Parenting. Pies for tonight's potluck.

And then time runs out. The day ends. Our lives end as well…before we meet all our deadlines.

One of my significant deadlines was a book contract for *Out of the Mouths of Grandbabes*. Our children had given us eight grandchildren who surprised us with God-messages out of the innocence of their littleness. Stories that needed to be written down, I thought, a self-imposed deadline before these little ones aged out of their uninhibited creativity. I also thought the births were over. Months after I had met the deadline, baby Isabel came into our lives. Even though the first deadline had been filled with stress, challenge, and angst, I longed for another one that would include her. Later the publishing agent phoned, "You aren't finished yet. We need an epilogue before we can go to print." Isabel got her tiny entry point into the book, but it was at the very end. Not exactly complete coverage.

G. K. Chesterton's poem gives me hope:

Now dies another day
With ear, hand, eye, world around me.
Tomorrow is another day.
Why am I given two?

Because, G. K., the generous God who extends our days on earth also beckons us into an infinity of numberless days. There will always be another day. Using myself up to meet daily deadlines is not my identity. I am a today-and-tomorrow-and-forever recipient of a lifeline. Damn the deadlines! Eternity is without them.

Sketch and write your own lines

FAVORITE LINES

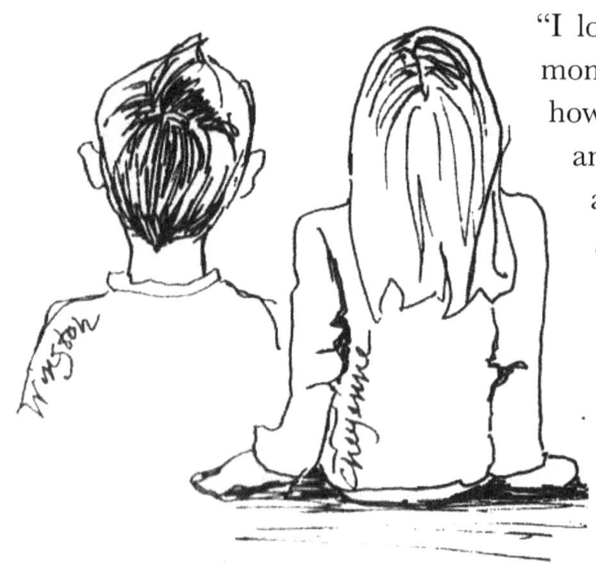

My favorite line of all time, written or spoken, would be absolutely true and purely understood. Is that even possible? Even when someone simply says, *I love you*, its meaning is fraught with complexities of doubt or disbelief, of wondering about motives, *or maybe right now you do, but just wait until I disappoint you.*

"I love you." A favorite line that says, for this moment at least, you are my favorite. Oh, how we long to be someone's favorite. Forever and always. It's the stuff of love stories, this affirmation that *You are my one and only. I only have eyes for you. You are the center of my universe.*

Humanly speaking, you can say all the 'favorite lines' another wants to hear, but you cannot deliver. Not continually and constantly. Your focus on your favorite person wanes and changes as distractions pile up and moods seep in. We even go so far as to say that God is our favorite, that we love Him above all else, but we forget about Him most of the day.

Truth be told, from my selfish, myopic, needy viewpoint, I fear I am not anyone's favorite. I want to be the always adored favorite of my husband, the favorite aunt, or grandmother, the favorite speaker at a conference, the favorite author, or, at the very least, someone's very best friend.

For over a decade I had the unpredictable and privileged position of counseling teenagers. For most of them, it was a time of plummeting self-esteem spiraled by a driving desire to be loved, or at least liked, and perhaps even popular. When someone announced on a given day, "You are my best friend," all the world became a glorious stage where favoritism dressed up as "you're okay; I'm okay." But days later, when you overheard the same someone talk about going with his or her best friend to a concert (and it wasn't you), the deflation of spirit became a drama of trying to figure out the lie of BFF (Best Friends Forever).

We brainstormed together about another way to be the best kind of friend. Suppose God really does decide when and where He places people? Suppose He chose when you would be born, for your parents to move to this town, send you to this school…because then you would meet these teenagers, these friends in this time and place? Daily divine encounters.

Imagine God auditioning and casting for the script He has written, so that you and a special someone would be onstage together. Your job is to make one another look good…to 'limelight' this friend in a love-beam. And then another crazy character enters stage right, and you do the same thing…help the spotlight land on them. This may be the key to all relationships…to focus on the one in front of you. To love with abandonment; to make each person the favorite right then and there. God chooses each of us to enter a stage in each other's stories and be messengers of His favorite line, spoken with feeling:

You are loved!

Every person is God's favorite.

Sketch and write your own lines

↓

FAULT LINES

What irony that an easy decision is dubbed a "no-brainer." An easy decision would be whether I want my life based on solid ground or shifting sands. "Solid ground," I would say without hesitation. But my brain generates questions: What kind of foundation brings a person peace and purpose? Who or what is in control here? How can I keep everyone safe? Including myself? Might I also need 'shifting sands' to generate change, develop flexibility, and grow empathy in me? Is there such a thing as 'total trust?'

Hmmm…no firm explanations. I thought my choices, easy or difficult, decided the direction of my life, a predictable path timeworn with the clarity of intellectually answered questions. But emotions are brain-based as well. When rational answers are elusive, their absence invites fear to walk our neuropaths with us. Ernest Becker says in *The Denial of Death* there is "the rumble of panic underneath everything."

Earthquakes wait to happen. Fault lines leave clues in the earth's crust that this ground is not solid and never has been. Fault lines, splitting through rocks, prove upheaval exists. Fault lines evoke fear—when will the next traumatic event shift and shake our lives to the core? We are cracked open when a sister dies young. A child is born disabled. An accident kills. Coffins come home from relentless wars. A marriage is on the rocks. A church splits. Corruption severs good in high places. Abuse happens.

We are left with a helplessness that defaults toward hopelessness. Timothy Keller, in his book *Walking with God through Pain and Suffering*, writes: "No amount of money, power, and planning can prevent bereavement, dire illness, relationship betrayal, financial disaster, or a host of other troubles from entering your life. Human life is fatally fragile and subject to forces beyond our power to manage. Life is tragic."

Perhaps we could just figure out what or who to blame. Whose fault are the fault lines? But often, blaming others for the damage is a game that very few win. And when we blame ourselves for the dark parts of our stories (those fault lines that divide our very souls) and get stuck in the crevasse of self-blame, our inward terrain is littered and embittered with the aftershock of pity and regret.

If we knew where to aim our pointing finger, we could obliterate the source of our traumas and heartbreak, eliminate the earthquakes and their accompanying fault lines, make the ground beneath our lives smooth and sure. "An act of God," the insurance companies say. And logic answers, "Then let's get rid of God!"

No God. Let my brain shock-struggle over that decision for a while. Obliterate God? (As if we could.)

I recall the biblical story of Elijah, who felt acute despair over God's absence. *A hurricane wind ripped through the mountains and shattered the rocks, but God wasn't to be found in the wind; after the wind an earthquake, but God wasn't in the earthquake; and after the earthquake, fire, but God wasn't in the fire; and after the fire a gentle and quiet whisper. At last, Elijah knew God was near through a still, small voice… — I Kings 19:9–12*

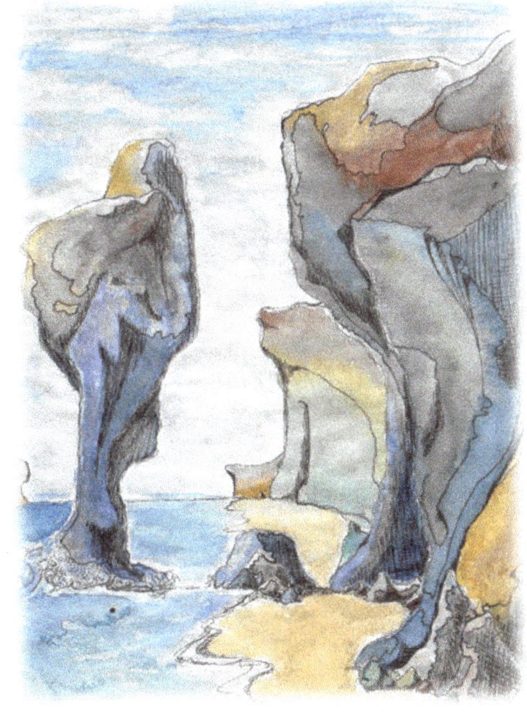

Hmmm…It seems God exists to provide unforeseen antidotes and cures for all that has ever gone terribly awry. To survive during and after every unexpected shake-up of our lives, we need the God who creates gentle and lovely things from a supernatural storehouse…and then outsources them to us. Quiet and powerful mysteries like healing, love, joy, peace, tenacity, goodness, compassion, loyalty, trust, enthusiasm, creativity, and purpose. Our boggled brains are unable to manufacture love and healing. Peace and joy do not evolve through millions of years; they start all over again in every newborn. God customizes goodness and grace and purpose to perfectly match the uniqueness of each person and experience. He is the bringer of life to each of us.

Our human concoctions of insurance policies will fail us in the end. Timothy Keller adds this: "At the most practical level, we have the crucial assurance that even wickedness and tragedy, which we know was not part of God's original design, is nonetheless being woven into a wise plan. So, the promise of Romans 8, 'that all things work together for good,' is an incomparable comfort to believers."

No God? We would also be eliminating the Creator of no-fault assurance. The kind of assurance where God takes on the blame for all that is horribly wrong in our world. Assurance that all damages have been covered and paid for when He died for us. This is the hope that enters our helplessness amid suffering.

Erase the God who can make the afflicted glad by turning ashes into beauty? (Ps. 34 and Isaiah 61:3) Get rid of the God who is the only source of life and resurrection? There is no One else who can make those things happen.

Hmmm…the final answer? I, for one, would like to keep God, if only for this: That in the end, when all fear-quaking and earth-shaking is over, we will be safe and alive with Him in a fault-free eternity.

Sketch and write your own lines ↓

FOWL LINES

My husband comes in from his 'chicken run.' "Another chicken is molting," he announces. "They don't lay eggs when they molt. Wonder what it is: not enough water; too low on the pecking order; seasonal?"

When I am in dialogue with members of my peer group (sexagenarians, septuagenarians, octogenarians), I sense we are sitting around molting. We talk about our shedding moments, realizations that substantial things are dropping out of our lives. Lesser losses are the small feathers in our caps. Overall, the molting changes are monumental. Gone are the jobs that gave us identity status, our kids whose rearing gave us purpose, and our once agile bodies that now betray us. Our former homes have morphed into a down-sized version, our material goods are ending up in garage sales, our brains often 'lose it', our own parents and several friends have died. Much can be checked off as 'Done.' We are looking at our feathers lying on the floor, left to deal with yellowing, saggy ugliness, unprotected and exposed.

Unless…unless we can reframe the chicken coop scenario into thankful memories of how productive we once were, God's grace and gifts to us by the dozens. Or a resurrection thought that after the molting is the promise of an immortal body, exquisitely perfect.

It helps me to think of doves rather than chickens. During our courting years, my husband affectionately called me 'DoVe'…a clever combination of the two letters of my first and maiden names before I changed my last name to his. Part of our love story.

The dove symbol throughout Christian history has stood for the Holy Spirit because a white one landed on Jesus' head when God spoke directly of His love for His Son. A dove reflects beloved-ness and loveliness…burdenless gifts that are feather-light. Chickens…not so much. Makes me want to shoo my older friends out of the chicken coop and into the dovecote.

I holler "Foul!" Then, having their attention, I line up my favorite fowl, these saintly aging doves, and remind us all how beautiful we are. Like Mary who was chosen to carry the baby Jesus, we have been chosen to carry His Spirit within.

We do not molt.

We fly!

Sketch and write your own lines

FUZZY LINES

We long to be sure.

We want our pasts to have true perspective, our living-in-the-present to be full of insightful mindfulness, and our futures to be clear. But our personal story lines seem fuzzy at best.

Describing the stories we tell of our past, Kat McGowan writes in a scientific journal featuring the brain: "As you replay…memories, you reawaken and re-consolidate them hundreds of times. Each time, you replace the original with a slightly modified version. Eventually you are not really remembering what happened; you are remembering your story about it." Our pasts become fuzzy as we embellish them with the telling.

The present? Who among us knows what is really happening when it is happening?

And then there is the future. We like to think we write the script. That there is a control factor about deciding one's own destiny. Or that expectant faith will somehow make things happen.

When I look ahead, I have no idea—not even a blurry one—about how the rest of my story will play out. Maybe all our stories can be categorized under the genre *Mystery*. Not only because we cannot immediately understand or solve the pile-up of daily details, but because what shapes our lives is unseen and immeasurable. There is mystery in how life begins, how relationships work, how healing and forgiveness take place, how transformation happens. And how can one explain love or hope or wonder? Mysteries, all.

When I look back on eight decades of experience, my overwhelming thought is: Surprise! God got me through SOMEHOW. It's the one thing in my story I feel the least fuzzy about. He was the one who brought people into my life like deliberate chess moves, epiphanies from out of nowhere, encouragement when the bottom was falling out, jobs when needed, coincidences falling like confetti, purposefulness and possibility threaded throughout my story line. Even details of these goodnesses sometimes get lost in memory fog.

I put SOMEHOW into my computer's search engine. A list of 925 synonymous words and phrases shows up. That large number reflects how ambiguous life is for all of humanity. We see through a lens of fuzzy lines. SOMEHOW has a host of unclear meanings: *one way or another, bizarrely, in some manner, how on earth? for some unknown reason, in a weird way, kinda, I know not why, whatever, etcetera*…and 916 more.

Buried in the middle of that list, somewhere around the 500 mark, is the phrase: *god knows*. The 'G' is not even capitalized. It first reads like a flippant cuss word. But then, it rises from its fuzzy-list grave and shouts the meaning of life to me and to a wishful world: God knows!

SOMEHOW the God of the universe, the God of us, is sure of what He is doing. God is God. He names himself I AM…present in the present, an unexplained "with-ness" that envelops our past and future into a "now" and an "always." And then, in His book, he writes this about Himself: "God is Love." The theory of relationship; the most mysterious equation ever.

God is God and God loves me. Two absolute truths and un-fuzzy lines. Out of them comes every SOMEHOW built into the complexities and surprises, the mysteries and miracles, of each of our lives.

SOMEHOW He has my back even though I felt misunderstood today; somehow He will fulfill the dreams of our son who didn't get the hoped for funding that his non-profit needs right now; somehow He will comfort the friends whose daughter just died tragically; somehow He has healing in mind for the neighbor who emailed this morning about the hits and misses of her bipolar condition; somehow He will figure out how to write the nations into a history that ends His way; somehow He will save the world. All our unfolding story lines are made clearer because of the certainty of God's unfailing presence.

Somehow the adverb SOMEHOW, fuzzy though it seems, enlarges my faith. Because for God…SOMEHOW is a sure thing.

Sketch and write your own lines ⟶

GUIDELINES

We need our life's journey clearly mapped out with a thick felt pen line. We want to know where we are going, making predictability synonymous with comfort and safety. Limbo is not the name of a destination. Planning, we assume, will guarantee satisfactory outcomes. Every time.

Can we really, by an act of our will, plan predictability into our lives if we follow certain guidelines? The definition of "guidelines" leaves some wiggle room. Rather than straightforward commands, guidelines are suggestions laced with hope, pieces of random advice, or a few instructions that call for additional creativity. Vague and generic, guidelines await a personalizing of the path ahead.

I loved my job as a high school counselor primarily because of its unpredictability. I could schedule appointments, but the predictability ended as soon as that personality walked in my office door. A senior boy came in one day and said he wanted to share his epiphany. Ahhh, the goodness of self-guidance shows up in a guidance counselor's office. He had just moved to the area, bringing with him an unsettledness of family dynamics, lack of motivation, and depression. But his grades improved, and he was playing baseball again, largely because a group of junior boys had befriended him. His epiphany moment? To do an extra year of high school by joining that junior class that had gifted him with belonging. He wanted to become more grounded before venturing on. Who saw that one coming?

Always, there seems to be a fork in the path…or several of them. Robert Frost has famously written: "Two roads diverged in a wood…" If you read the entire poem, you discover that even though he is glad he chose the less-traveled path, he still longs to know where the other path would have taken him. We want guidance to point to the exact opportunity best for us so that when we leave the plethora of other possibilities behind, we have no regrets. But that is our conundrum: we never know.

Sometimes, without clear guidelines, we simply wander, zigzag, or even get stuck for a while. We are left with trust in the God of mystery and miracle. "Which is when," a young friend of mine says, "I cross over that bridge to somewhere, and figure it out along the way, praying and trusting as I go." There are mile markers and road signs ahead, much like guidelines except that we do not receive them ahead of time. They are down the road and out of sight, waiting, proving God's 'thereness' even when we thought we were running blind. Sometimes God blazes trails for us where we can barely make out a path through the brambles and tangles; sometimes He paves the way so we can make good time at freeway speeds.

Remember those pages in our childhood coloring books that instructed us to connect the dots? Divine guidelines seem more dot-like than one thick, black line across the map of our lives. If we follow the numbers, an image unfolds, unpredictable and surprising, but satisfying. We keep going because we can trust our God-given visibility for a few feet ahead…to the next dot. Dot by dot, God gives us guidelines, mile markers, epiphanies, and signposts:

- a word from God's Word
- the perfectly timed encouragement
- a prayer
- sunset awe
- triggered tears
- that stranger who walks toward you across a crowded room and into your life
- an insight about a decision
- the coincidences that land you a job
- a pregnancy
- that dream in your sleep of God's everlasting arms carrying you in your grief
- when a counselor, a friend, or the Spirit shows up
- a hug full of warm love

Lots and lots of dots.

Guidelines turn out to be dotted lines, an unfolding journey of the most unpredictable kind. Here is your pencil. Just start connecting the dots…. It's fun; you'll see.

Sketch and write your own lines ⟶

HAIRLINES

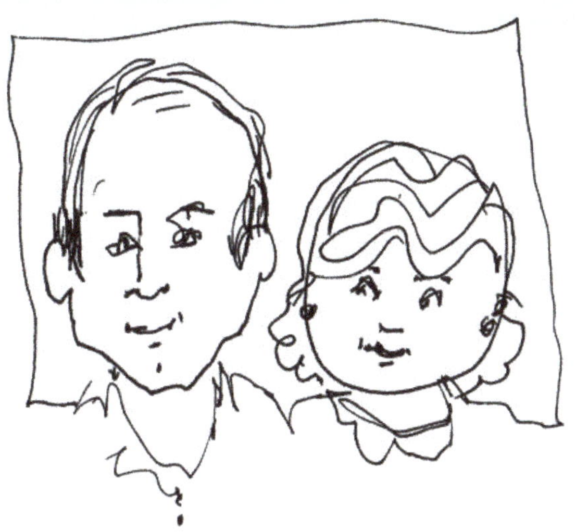

My sister and her husband describe their foreheads thusly: His is a 5-head (significantly receding hairline); hers is a 3-head (not much space between eyebrows and hairline). They joke that together they average out to a 4-head.

Because they are so front and center, we pay a lot of attention to hairlines. Endless choices exist for making them cute or handsome: stand-up hair, moussed to a sculptural perfection, or sweeping bangs playing tag with one's eyelashes; fastidiously even sideburns or the feathered-around-the-face look; dye-colored for a conspicuous hairline or obliterate it altogether by completely shaving one's head.

Our three sons have deep and wide bald furrows receding back from their foreheads, leaving an M-shaped hairline, the middle of which points to their nose. Their father and both their grandfathers had full heads of hair, no furrows. DNA studies of baldness have turned to the maternal grandmother as the carrier. But their Grandma Flo had a lifetime of thick hair, and her only brother never became bald. The sketchy science on hairlines has been called a "genetics myth."

A middle school principal was dealing with an 8th grader who was "behaviorally challenged." There was tension in the principal's office: patient explanation of consequences on one side, but rebellion and anger on the other. Awkward silences. Finally, feeling punishment was totally unwarranted, the adolescent shouted, "This just isn't fair!" Without a blink in his eye-to-eye contact, the principal said to the lad, "David, if life was fair, I would have hair." Another long silence…and then a burst of laughter. "Mr. Baines, you've got me there." And off he went, cooperatively and sympathetically, to after-school detention.

Remember Yul Brynner? Considered one of the first Russian American film stars, he shaved his head for the role in *The King and I* in 1951. Legendary as much for his bald head as for his acting, Yul paved the way for baldness being considered sexy. Decades later, Google entries have confused the issue: "Studies have been inconsistent across cultures about how balding men rate on the attraction scale. While a South Korean study showed that most people rated balding men as less attractive, a survey of Welsh women found that they rated bald and gray-haired men quite desirable."

Hairlines, though their significance is confusing and small, are so very obvious. They get in our face and often bother us. Like dust balls or peeling paint, they have a way of catching one's attention, nagging for elimination or a solution: cut your hair; shave your neck; curl the straight; straighten the frizz. During the pandemic's isolation, when we couldn't solve our head problems by going to a barber or a hair salon, we stayed home, did a bit of self-whacking, and reflected even as our hair kept growing….

Jesus turned the truth-about-hair on its head for me when He said: *the very hairs of your head are numbered*. One morning, feeling particularly limited and non-essential in this 'elderly vulnerable at-risk' category, I needed those words about hairs on our heads and lilies and sparrows…how they don't strive but simply exist, how He notices those small entities and values them immensely. How everything counts somehow. He reminded me that I still have the capacity to notice, to praise, and to enjoy. To do the quiet, un-dramatic acts that no one, including me, thinks will change the world. I noticed my Mother's Day marigold plant that was dying yesterday had come alive. It helped that I watered it… And my husband, who was sick the last few days, is feeling better. Perhaps the caregiving, minimal as it was, urged him on. Later came a Spirit-thought: *just email Emily. Begin with*, "It's been a while. I need connection…and maybe you do, too. Care comes alive in me when I think of you…and so does curiosity. How are you?" *And finish with a few lines about hair that you learned from Me today.* Later she wrote back. "Your words were like honey to my little storm-tossed soul. Thank you for being faithful to reach out and check in."

The God of the universe wants us to know that the hairs on our heads (or each whisker on our chins if you are bald like Mr. Baines or Mr. Brynner) are safely within His purview. And that He works those tiny strands imaginatively into His epic narrative about us all. Hairlines figure into making jokes, shaping adolescent boys, staging musicals, providing practice for at-home haircuts, and even showing up in biblical metaphors. But you, Jesus concludes, *you are much more valuable than these*….

What I know now is this: My heart holds love and meaning, not my hairline.

Sketch and write your own lines ⟶

FAMILY LINES

After we were home again, a young friend asked me, "So…how was your family reunion?"

"Good!" said I. "We all came home alive!"

She laughed and said, "That's a pretty low bar of expectation for a family gathering."

This was a conversation "in passing." Had there been more time, as a grandmother in reunion recovery, I might have said this in my defense: I sincerely do not want to be that annoying wart of worry that shows up during family doings and ruins God's open-handed gift of time together. But we were in the Montana wilderness after all. Our grandkids swam in a lake that is deep and has sinkholes and leeches, crawled through a cold-numb mountain stream against the current, fished the river, did no-hand gymnastic flips on hard, dry ground, drove four-wheelers, and hacked out paths through the woods. They saw the red ant hill as big as a bushel basket soon enough to avoid it; but not the yellow jacket nest (a grandson took eight stings for the team). Not to mention the grizzly sightings in the area that generated the buddy system and cans of bear spray on board.

The grandmotherly concern I have for our nine grandchildren seems to have ratcheted up a few notches from the motherly care I experienced with our children. Perhaps it's because there are so many more of them to fret over. Or as one grandfather put it, "I knew my own so well, I could usually predict and trust what they were going to do. I'm not in my grandchildren's lives that closely or that daily, so the unknowns tend to move me toward worry."

Or maybe it's because the stories pile up over the decades and lodge in some folder of our brain's memory bytes, stories of accidents and tragedies, suicides and mental illnesses that happen to the young. At our recent reunion, an uncle shared the story of a graduation pool party that took place in his California town with a hundred guests and a couple of lifeguards present where a four-year-old drowned unnoticed. That's when my grandma pleas become, "Please, God, Noooo!" A tragedy happening to a beloved grandchild is an unimaginable, unthinkable thought.

The love piles up, too, over the decades. We grow more and more fond of each of the four kids we housed through their growing years as they become more and more of who God intended them to be apart from us. Our children's preciousness is simply more precious to us. And then they marry and do this miraculous thing of presenting us with in-laws and grandchildren to love. Those deep and generational loves want ever so much to keep the hurt away. We want our families to experience shalom, a flourishing in all things physical and psychological and spiritual.

Meanwhile the world seems bent on becoming a scarier place. Maybe every older generation sees it that way, but have you noticed that these days extreme sports have become more extreme, drugs more dangerous, alcohol more plentiful, mental illness more rampant, sexual behavior more damaging, divides more unbridgeable, and violence more in-your-face?

So why do we have a family reunion year after year in that same Montana acreage? Because it is a 'thin place' in God's geography where the divide between heaven and earth is hardly discernable, where creation's beauty becomes a revelation of God Himself, where silence is really solitude that can feel the "more" of a divine presence. Have I mentioned there is no internet? We play and enjoy one another and feel God's pleasure in His generosity to this one small family. "This place and these people are in the hearts of your grandchildren," one daughter-in-law commented. "It is part of their souls."

There is always risk on God's good earth…and danger. Creation is the PowerPoint presentation that shows us how to embrace all that God has for us while trusting Him to take care of us. Letting myself love means setting myself up—for risk, for loss, but also for joy.

Worry may be a good thing after all—the very trigger God uses to remind us that He welcomes every hollered and every whispered prayer that comes from our helpless hearts.

Rejoice in the Lord always.
Don't fret or worry. Instead of worrying, pray.
Let petitions and praises shape your worries into prayers,
letting God know your concerns.
Before you know it, a sense of God's wholeness,
everything coming together for good,
will come and settle you down.
It's wonderful what happens when Christ displaces worry
at the center of your life.
— Phil. 4:4-7

Sketch and write your own lines ⟶

LAUGH LINES

Have you ever noticed that approximately half of humanity features a mouth that turns down at the corners, on its way to a frown…while the other 50% have mouths that turn slightly upward toward a smile? Consider first impressions. We project the frown or smile emoji on someone we have just met by reading those lip lines, label a person as either negative or positive, sad or happy, worried or relaxed, slightly angry or pretty content.

I carry the downward curve on my face; I have suffered from first impression discrimination and been victimized by emoji labeling. And just now, reading that sentence, you are thinking *what a 'downer' she must be!* But really, I was trying to be funny. I have been asked, *Is something bothering you?* or told, *You look tired, or droopy* when in reality I felt relaxed and energized. The assessment of my wrinkles while in my coffin will probably not be, *Look at those laugh lines!* But I want it to be so.

I suspect fewer than half of humanity laughs out loud, an exercise which would, no doubt, deepen one's laugh lines. My guess would be that 80% guffaw or giggle very privately within themselves, which regrettably renders most forms of laughter un-contagious. I remember observing a mischievous classmate in the school library hidden behind the bookcases reading comic books and laughing out loud. Sixty years later that fond memory remains, captioned by my smiling heart: *Go, thou, and do likewise.*

The best kind of laughter bubbles uncontainably, bursting corks out of champagne bottles. My husband and I (of stoic, serious, northern European descent) have decided to uncap a little more, practice laughing out loud. No longer do we watch M.A.S.H. reruns without making a joyful noise. We uncork and chuckle noisily upon hearing a pun (Our mountains aren't just funny; they're hill areas.) or a joke (Life is short. If you can't laugh at yourself, call me. I will). How empty life would be without the lines that make us laugh!

My friend and her sister took their 89-year-old mother to the state transportation department, not to renew her driver's license, but for a wallet I.D. They had a long wait, time for much bantering and repeated primping on her part. "This is an important photo shoot for me, you know," she told her girls with a grin on her face. "Why?" they asked. "Because I'm thinking it will do for my obituary picture." Together they laughed heartily. From whence comes this freedom to see hilarity in death?

Long ago I discovered a portrait of *The Laughing Jesus*, unframed and dust-laden, on a hard-to-get-at shelf in the corner of a used bookstore. I was "taken" by it…and since then, influenced by it…just as any artist hopes his or her work will do. I thought the artist wanted anonymity because the portrait was not signed, but an internet search showed that a Canadian named Willis Wheatly sketched and painted it over 40 years ago, artistically including those divinely human or humanly divine laugh lines.

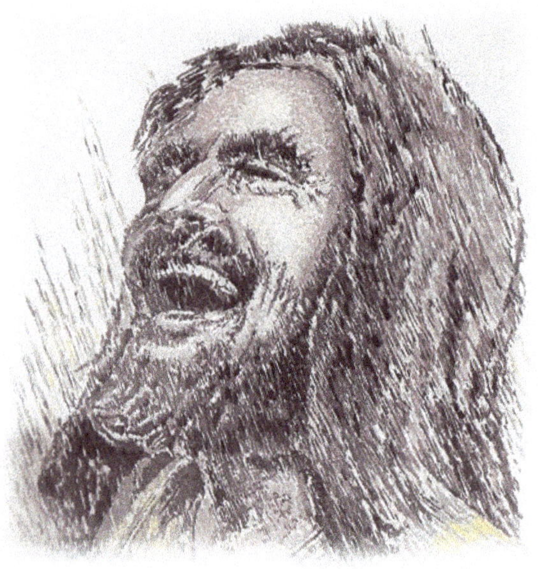

We placed the portrait centrally in our *living room* (whoever coined that phrase imagined us *living* fully in that space with couches by firesides, books on tables, and lively conversations, a way of "practicing resurrection" together). Seeing Jesus with His head back in full-throated laughter helps me appreciate him as someone fully alive, as someone who delights in the entire human race. Out of His agony in dying for us comes this surprising truth: *because of the joy that was set before Him, He endured the cross…* — *Hebrews 12:6* Jesus was moved from near paralysis to profound purpose by a joy that pictured you, that knew about me. Clearly, He wanted laugh lines to replace our tears.

Sketch and write your own lines ⟶

LIFELINES

What do we do the morning after? The morning after our teen-aged nephew's death?

I have a persisting memory of the morning after my too-young sister died years ago. I felt repelled by breakfast crumbs and dirty dishes on the table; everything in me rebelled against doing the ordinary tasks of eating and cleaning. I wanted to kick table legs, overturn that table, angry about dealing with the mundane in the face of such monumental loss…

But this morning, grieving our nephew's untimely death, the last story of John's gospel lodges in me.

"Come and have breakfast," Jesus invites.

So, the disciples came ashore for fried fish cooked by their Lord who had started the fire, brought the pan, and provided some bread. They ate together…and cleaned up.

Together they also turn the ordinary into the holy as they spend time together. The conversation starts with a question.

"Do you love me?" Jesus asks one of them. Even when all of them are reeling from His death, sunk in the heaviness of loss and confusion, "Do you love me?" becomes central.

While eating toast and chewing on fish, processing thoughts within this ordinary morning, one disciple's declaration becomes a hesitant 'yes.' And then, with more discussion and grappling, even some agonizing, Peter finally ends with a resounding "Yes! You know that I love you."

More talking ensues…about how the death of one of His own glorifies God. More attempts at wrapping their minds around that truth. More 'holy conversation'…

As the campfire dies down, Jesus simply says to them, "Follow me." Clear guidance on this foggy morning…a lifeline that fills their remaining earth-lives with meaning and purpose. And when each heart stops, the lifeline pulses on, pulling us into the forever rescue of resurrection.

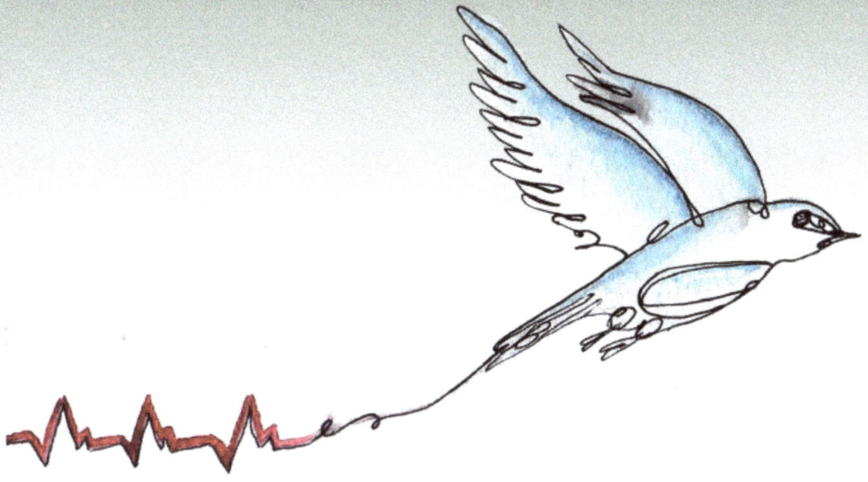

This grief-filled morning, in chronological time, Jesus breakfasts with us, invites us into His love, brings us together, calls us to talk with Him and about Him, and urges us to say "Yes!" to each new day. He is alive and timeless! And so are we!

Sketch and write your own lines

↓

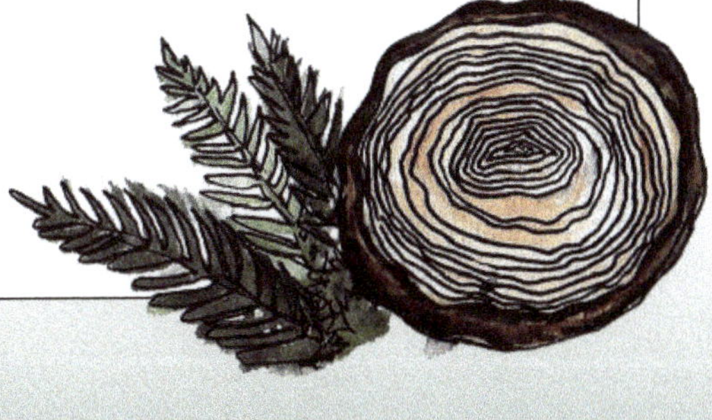

LINEAR THINKING

My husband and I find ourselves in the middle of a January-term course with college students, invited along as retirees for a monastic learning experience. We hide the joy that may be perceived as giddy immaturity….

We sat down together and ate the breaded fish sticks offered from the camp's kitchen at our spiritual retreat site. We tasted the same loaf-and-fish menu that Jesus miraculously served when He fed the 5000. Same entrees, different presentations. But we didn't experience the meal as supernatural…in fact, we gave it very little thought. Our thinking went into the table discussion that followed:

"If God has foreknowledge of everything that happens, where is our free will?" asks one of the theology students.

"If every decision we make is shaped by all the accumulated experiences we have had up to that point, do we have any control over our own lives?" asks another.

The responses come quickly: "Maybe life is like that exercise we do with dominos where our first experience affects the next and that one affects the next, each one toppling into a forward movement until there's a little glitch of spacing. Maybe it's then that we need an outside source to recalibrate so that we don't stay stuck. Then God breaks through, reorganizes the domino chain, and someone's story has a Damascus Road that moves one in another direction."

"Isn't that determinism?" someone asks. "And do we really believe in that?"

"What about predestination?"

The discussion meanders down several paths. A collegiate on my right whispers, "This is what academia is like. Don't you just love it?!"

My mental muscles trigger into memory mode. College was like that…even fifty years ago. We engaged excitedly in the freedom and opportunity to ask the hard questions. We considered ourselves quite unbelievably brave for entertaining those we thought everyone else was avoiding. We even felt the rush of reaching conclusions (maybe for the first time in history?!) In our youthful and idealistic approach, we failed to see that some of our answers might be wrong, so dangerously wrong, in fact, that they could lead us away from the truth instead of finding it.

Another student chimes in: "We cannot be rational about everything. Two of my friends have given up their faith because they intellectually could not find answers. They've come up empty."

As humans we seem prone to linear thinking, the kind that wants categories and closures, where going in a straight line from point A to point B will result in solutions, where six or seven simple and logical steps will change one's life. We draw lines between things and people, developing our own little multiple-choice world. We take sides. Is God A. my father…or B. my judge?

ABBA is the name He asks His children to call Him. God incorporates both A and B rather than just one or the other. He can supernaturally unify what we see as division into a wonder of wholeness. He mysteriously melds the human and divine qualities in Jesus. He takes our human wills and meshes them with His foreknowledge. He sorrows and rejoices over us. He delights in and fully embraces ethnic and cultural differences.

He is a both/and God, not an either/or One. Our unfathomable God goes far beyond logic and linear thinking.

The God equation I remember best from the Bible: God is Love. Love always unifies, never separates. All the lines of either/or are removed; all the pressing choices of an A or a B are gone. Abba engulfs us with the both/and of an inclusive circle of endless, irrational Love.

Come to think of it, perhaps our breaded fish meal was both natural /*and* supernatural, both miracle /*and* ordinary. Like undeserved mystery manna we didn't prepare ourselves coming daily from *both* the heart *and* hand of our God.

Sketch and write your own lines ⟶

LINES OF POETRY

The following poem touched me recently:

On Growing Old
A time will come to sit in the shadow of these trees,
shawls on our laps, too old even to remember our names.
So let's try this. Let's write "Holy, Holy, Holy, Holy"
on old scraps of paper and fold them tightly into tiny pills.
For whatever Light awaits us on the other side, surely
it can't hurt to have some praises already on our tongues.

Father Zosima

My strongest emotion while immersed in slowly reading the poem was calm toward a long dying. I have vivid memories of visiting my mother in the Alzheimer's unit where nearly everyone had a lap blanket and couldn't remember their names or those of their children. The poem places the 'old ones' outside under a tree…together…and then gives them something to do using words and paper scraps, an action that counteracts their helplessness.

When I put myself in that scene, the blanket becomes my Comforter, the outdoors reflects God's creative presence, and being in community always blesses me. It gave me a more positive picture of this aging toward imminent reality. I felt warmth on my lap, fresh air in my lungs, my eyes opened to God's wonders…all while in good company.

I re-read these lines of poetry. And then I sigh. I have never praised God enough. Relief comes to me as a writer who's always searching for the best words, editing endlessly, working the phrases to get just the right meaning. But the poem says, "Just write HOLY"…it contains all the praise meanings in one word, even if written on scraps and scrunched into pills. I have also struggled with whether taking medications might be a lack of faith. The poem elevates pill-taking, turning it to praise.

The last line takes away the "hurt" of unavoidable death, turning it into a happy-to-finally-be-here reunion with God, full of exuberant worship of the partying kind. The poet's final commentary "…surely it can't hurt to have some praises already on our tongues" makes me smile and relax with anticipation.

Which is God's message to us: smile, relax; I've got you covered.

Sketch and write your own lines

↓

LINING UP ALPHABETICALLY

I sometimes go through the alphabet naming the attributes of God and tossing them out and up for the ears of God. This exercise has a way of helping me muscle my way through the day, knowing Who it is that walks or runs or crawls beside me. **God, you are…**

Adorable. Forgive us, Lord, for morphing this attribute into all that is cute and shallow and tiny like the way we see our toddlers. We adore You! How can we "stand" in awe when we should be face-down prone before the God who made light years of time and the distances of the universe? A God who created a jillion individual people, then wrote page-turner stories about each of them, including Himself in each narrative. Your people adore You!

Beautiful. You are the source of all beauty. How do we even start the naming of this endlessness of creativity? Babies? The curl of their fingers, their baby breaths, the smooth and the soft of them, the wide-eyed taking in, the eyelashes and fingernails, the toe count, the cries that make a mother's uterus clench with the memory of who she has birthed, the future in someone so small…. You personify Beauty!

Compassionate. You are the Caregiver who knows me so well. You custom-make ways to show Your love specifically for me. Like in that simple walk on the beach this morning—I heard your nearness in the rhythmical music of waves that have kept their beat on that silent shore for eons; I felt Your tenderness when my tired feet were caressed by the soft white sand pulverized from rocks and seashells over thousands of years. I heard You through that church bell tolling to remind me of all the ways You love Your redeemed.

Divine, of course. Mysteriously holy; utterly capable. The hymn title Dona Nobis Pacem darts into my 'D' category, the chanting haunt of a melody playing on my memory bytes. Written during WWI by someone listening to God for a way to redeem the times…a prayer that cries: "Grant Us Peace." Only the Divine can obliterate the unholy causes for war and every other dissonance within each of us.

Elohim. This is how you introduced yourself to Moses, an epithet that means "I am that I am" and reflects an infinity of fullness and fulfillment. Our incompletes will all be canceled because of Who you are. (See "L")

Far. It is not You who are far away; it is You who have removed our sins far from us. Forgiveness has a far-away dimension to it of the disappearing kind.

Good. *"And God said, 'Let there be light.' And God saw that the light was good."* But before all that goodness: *"Earth was a soup of nothingness, a bottomless emptiness, an inky blackness."* — *Genesis 1.* Thank you for creating good Light for our earth-home.

Hosanna! Hallelujah! Heaven. Holy…good realities and soft shouts to get us through the Hard.

Incubator. You are the God of all birthing into all beginnings. The Creator of seed and life and womb and labor and awe. The Encourager of all growing things into the selfhood You created them to be. The Originator of thought and truth, of love and rescue. You are the One who cracks us open to receive.

Joy. On Friday…and every day before and thereafter. From Your joy comes ours: the joy of our salvation, the joy of discovery, the joy set before us to motivate our good deeds, the joy in seeing another joyful, the underlying joy and the tired joys of just plain living, the joy that bursts in on scenes of beauty, the joy in meaning, and even that unexplainable joy that comes out of suffering.

Kairos. You are above and beyond and outside of time as we know it in our chronological boundaries. How do you supersede our days, float through our hours, count a thousand years as one day, run creation by nanoseconds and eternal moments?

Love. "But for right now, until that completeness, we have three things to do: *Trust steadily in God, hope unswervingly, love extravagantly. And the best of the three is love."* —*I Corinthians 13.* You are Love, dear God. We count on You to love us, to generate that love in us for others and for ourselves. Only You can pass the Love around.

Mighty. I assign to You, O Lord, the ability to do extraordinary things in peoples' lives with an unexplainable power, sometimes quietly subtle and slow (as we humans measure time), sometimes surprisingly instant. I hope for miracles: I look for them; sometimes I even manage to expect them. I like the **Al**mighty word better— **All** might is yours.

Nailed. That suffering-on-the-cross? "Such a mind-boggling, heart-moving thing, God!" This we exclaim as we suck in our breaths and surrender to a sin solution that we would have never thought of or carried through.

Omnipresent. Omniscient. Omnipotent. My heart emits "Ohhh's" of awe as I consider these "O" words. It makes sense to worship a God who is everywhere, knows everything, and who is all-powerful.

Punitive. That You punish and eradicate evil deserves praise. That You use us to partner in seeking and preserving justice leaves us overwhelmed without You. That you have willed not to pay us our sin wages, but to do a mercy-purchase for our souls…for all these we praise You!

Quotidian. Never!
Quotable. Always!

Righteous. In the middle of the third chapter of Romans: *"The God-setting-things-right that we read about has become Jesus-setting-things-right for us."* The finality of that makes me free. That "getting it right," being righteous as You are righteous, is Your gift, not my achievement.

Spontaneous. Because You have an infinite plan, because Sovereign is Your name, because fore-thought and after-thought are unnecessary for a timeless God, because You have no baggage and always function freely…for this we praise You! We love the ways You show up in the circumstances and coincidences of our lives. Was it You "messaging" me on my walk through that hefty woman with chartreuse shoestrings in her shoes? Smiling, she shouted a very bold Good Morning! as we passed one another…maybe mimicking Your desire for me that day. We both loop back and meet again, so I say, "We're doin' it!" and she says, "Yes, we are!" Spontaneous encouragements out of Your random kindness to one woman hoping to counteract weight gain and another wanting to stave off arthritic stiffening.

Truth. "What is truth?" we humans ask. *"I am the Truth,"* Jesus truthfully reveals.

Uninhibited. There is no fear in You! You fling stars across the whole universe without worrying about whether they will stay or explode. You keep making babies knowing that You have enough perfect love to cast out the fear in each life story. You orchestrate sunrises and sunsets that never repeat each other. You add and mix the colors on Your creation canvas without listening to Your inner critic because that is non-existent in You.

Valiant. By Your courage we are saved. And then You ask us, too, to be brave…to do battle along with You. And You give us our own shining armor: the belt of truth, the breastplate of righteousness, the footwear of readiness that comes from the gospel of peace, the shield of faith, the helmet of salvation, and the sword of the Spirit (the latter being Your very Word to us). May these provisions make us fearless.

The Waiter. We praise You for waiting on us. First, You serve us and then…You are patient with us…waiting. These are surprising things for a God. Your servant heart that embraces sacrifice to make us whole is astounding. We feast at a table with food for flourishing and wine for forgiveness. Your patience with our slow growth from such satisfying fare humbles us. And Your long waiting for what the Apostle Peter explains is incomprehensible to us: *"The Lord is not slow in keeping his promise, as some understand slowness. Instead, he is patient with you, not wanting anyone to perish, but everyone to come to repentance."*

Xero. This name of a former internet company reminds me of Your mathematical genius. Clever of them to spell zero with an 'X,' that symbol for "unknown" until we get it figured out, until all is bottom-line balanced, 0 to 0. You are our "unknown God," our mathematical mystery Who has solutions for every problem and has perfect balance amid all that doesn't add up.

Yahweh. Years ago, we had a buzz phrase for disbelief: 'No way!' We also said a slang 'Yeah' for 'Yes.' Every time I would hear Your name Yahweh, I would translate it into an affirmation of belief: Yes way!! You are the Way…the One who drank the full cup so that our realities would not be half empty.

Zed. All alphabets in every language on earth come to an end. Even with their nearly endless combinations of letters into words, and words into graphic scenes, abstract philosophies, song lyrics, and books…still there is always The End. With God there is no end. May we praise Him forever without end.

Sketch and write your own lines ⟶

LININGS

A tailor inserts a lining in a skirt or pants for modesty's sake. A cloud's silver lining becomes the encouragement to dream light-bright color into a gray world. One's stomach lining helps prevent ulcers. Protection appears as a theme here. An effective lining can save one from embarrassment or depression or pain.

And have you given any thought lately to those membrane linings around your heart? Three of them. Protection in triplicate. No messing around with this crucial muscle that keeps us alive. The Creator had "heart-healthy" in mind for each of us from the beginning. These heart linings are not layered like three cuts from the same cloth as if triple strength were all that was needed. Instead, the outside layer is a combination of spandex (to keep our heart from enlarging) and a tethered net (to keep it from moving around and losing its spot): Stability. The middle layer is a living lining of spark plugs that starts our rhythmic heart beats: Life-energy. The inner layer protects the chambers, valves, and vessels deep within the heart from intrusion or overload of outside forces: Security.

Stability. Life-energy. Security. These descriptions of the heart's three linings have a Trinity-feel about them: a lining for stability that assures our unique existence; a layer for energy to course life through us; and a lining for secure protection given by the God who loves us.

Linings of functional tissue protect the central pump that keeps us physically alive. But there are issues as well as tissues. A Psalmist writes this: *Above all, guard your heart, for out of it come the issues of life.* Beyond exporting and importing blood, the heart is credited with all things relational, psychological, and theological: thoughts, feelings, beliefs, values, self-knowledge, and finding God.

Our anatomical heart, when working well, cannot expand beyond its outer lining. But when we say, "He or she is all heart," we are describing someone who exudes generosity and love and wholeness. Our soul-and-spirit core is not a heart encased purely for function, but, at its most healthy, limitless and free. Eugene Peterson, in his book *Traveling Light*, writes that when we are saved and safe because our hearts have believed in redemption, we are free indeed. He writes about his own heart: "…when I live in faith I live freely. When I set God at the center of my life, I realize vast freedoms and surprising spontaneities. When I center life in my own will, my freedom diminishes markedly. I live constricted and anxious."

I thank God for physical linings that keep my heart in place and pumping, and for the psychological linings that keep me safe and secure…while I am earthbound. God does guard my heart, but He is not over-protective. His open invitation to me is stamped with **God is Love** and reads: *"Come home to Me, believe in Me, belong to Me."*

And I answer, "Here's my heart, Lord." It is in that Yes!-moment that my unconstricted heart expands beyond my imagination.

Sketch and write your own lines ↓

LYRICAL LINES

Let me explain how Tigger and Henry Nouwen turned up in my prayer life yesterday.

I was repeating a Psalm-prayer of David back to the God who inspired him. David had begged desperately for mercy, weeping into the night until his 'couch was drenched with his tears.' His final line promises *"the Lord has heard my supplication; the Lord accepts my prayer."*

My prayer was simple and mundane, not as pleading and passionate as David's, but laced with the belief that God not only listens, He also desires to answer requests from a child of His.

I needed an insight into God's will about whether to do a lecture or an interview for a women's ministry, which involved being videotaped for an online discipleship course entitled Women of Impact. God has been generous over so many decades with His opportunities for me to speak gospel to others, but…not only do my inadequacies loom (which He has mercifully overcome many a time), but my energy in this 'growing old' season has lessened considerably.

After morning prayers, during vibrations from my electric toothbrush, Tigger's lyrics flit through my thoughts: …

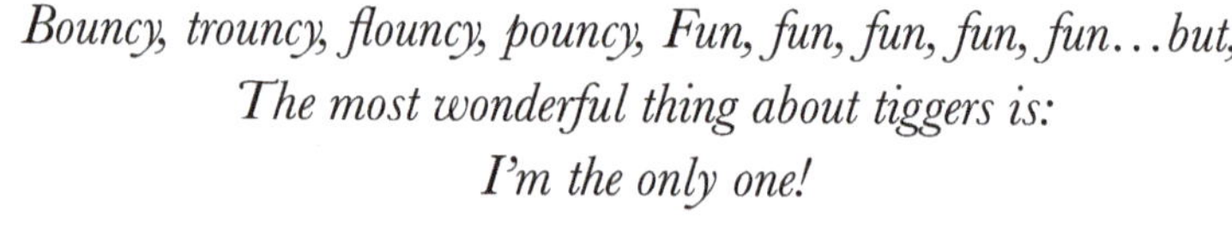

Bouncy, trouncy, flouncy, pouncy, Fun, fun, fun, fun, fun…but,
The most wonderful thing about tiggers is:
I'm the only one!

These lyrical lines describe a beloved cartoon character. Creative and delightful, yes. But factually a little off. There isn't *only one* that can inspire others. Phillip Yancey's article in *Christianity Today* (December 9, 1996) describes the one and only Henry Nouwen as Tigger-like: "…the energetic priest, hair in disarray, using his restless hands as if to fashion a homily out of thin air, celebrating an eloquent Eucharist…" But it was a later line that answered my prayerful sorting out: "Nouwen has said that all his life two voices competed inside him. One encouraged him to succeed and achieve, while the other called him simply to rest in the comfort that he was 'the beloved' of God. Only in the last decade of his life did he truly listen to that second voice."

Nouwen turned down speaking engagements and instead took care of Adam, a seriously disabled young man. "It had been difficult for me at first," he said. "Yet in the process I learned what it must be like for God to love *us*—spiritually uncoordinated,…able to respond with what must seem to God like inarticulate grunts and groans."

I feel God's tug to focus more on being rather than doing. No longer even a caricature of the high-energy Tigger, I am slowing to a rest-in-the Lord stop, sitting with the Psalms to love Him more and be reminded of His love for me. Instead of the bounce and flounce it takes to step up to a podium facing an audience, I now sit with one person at a time in my living room, walk with another, or drink coffee with a granddaughter.

Often, after dark, I face the still-water pond in our pasture and belt out those lyrical lines of the doxology with the frogs: *"Praise Him all creatures here below."* Sometimes God's will for you or me is to be a featured soloist in a frog chorus. Praise Him with singing!

Sketch and write your own lines

↓

MEASURING LINES

Assuming the new cookie recipe will call for some measuring, I reach for the glass Pyrex measuring cup with the red lines on it. Carefully I fill, shake and line up the sugar level to the ¾ cup mark on the side. I do the same with the flour. Dry measurements. Next the milk…noting the ounce lines, or the liters and milliliters. Liquid measurements. I try not to spill…

I remember a few years ago when it was a fad to begin the New Year with a one-word resolution. Intentionally crafting a whole sentence of self-improvement simply took too much time in our instant culture. So, I considered 'joy' or 'empathy' or 'awareness,' noble pursuits that they are. But the word 'cupful' nagged at me instead. I didn't even know it was one word; for sure I knew it was two: cup full. But when I typed 'cupful' into my computer, there was no red line to warn of a spelling error. Thus, it qualified as a one-word goal. I hoped to remember it until February.

I began saying it over and over: cupful, cupful, cupful. It began sounding like 'kerfuffle'… which means some kind of crazy combination of fuss and confusion…a dubious purpose to work on for an entire year.

But I had been thinking about chaos theory. Because as one gets older the illusion of being in control, of living a measured life by organizing outcomes, starts slipping away. The notion that one can avoid every kerfuffle, always steer clear of spilling, or even keep the messes cleaned up, becomes laughable. Maybe a little chaos is okay; perhaps God is even in charge of it.

The *"In the beginning"* announcement of existence from Genesis 1 has also been translated: *"When God began to create…the earth was formless, void, with deep waters covered in darkness."* There is something about that *when*, as if God was waiting, but poised and ready. Could it mean He had already prepared the raw materials for planet earth before He created our world as we know it? If so, He understands chaos. Which is why He could pull life and light from all that pre-planned disorder. *"Let there be Light!"* was His first call-out to the chaos. Then He decided to keep the darkness so that we could measure our days. After that God took unformed and lifeless dust, created a human out of that unlikely source, and breathed into it the *"breath of life."*

Chaos, then, has potential and beauty and surprises residing within it. Which means my daily kerfuffles can become cupfuls of awe, filling me with relief and gratitude for how God turns my "fuss and confusion," my heart and my circumstances, into art forms. And because Genesis 1 also says I am created in His image, I, too, can creatively work with my kerfuffles.

There are so many ways to take measure of a life, cupful by cupful. *My cup runneth over*, a famous Psalm writer says. Sounds like a spillover mess to me…until I understand it as a bountiful brimming of luxurious love gifts from a God whose generosity is endless.

Does your cup measurement read "half empty," registering a void of some kind? A creative soul made in God's image has said: "If your cup is half empty, pour it into a smaller cup and stop whining."

Sketch and write your own lines

MEMORIZED LINES

As children we memorized lines for roles in plays, for sing-alongs and joke-telling, lines from Scripture and poetry and pieces of music. We even remember some of them: *For God so loved the world… Old MacDonald had a farm… Jesus loves me this I know… Knock, Knock. Who's there?*

We have known the contractor who is renovating our basement for a long time, ever since he and our son were kindergarten buddies close to fifty years ago. He recalls being in our home, noting again the nooks and crannies where they played hide-and-seek, the laundry chute they slid through, and the windows they jumped out of. He brings back memories of the precocious twosome they once were. To make room for his remodel, we decided to chop up and burn the old pump organ that has lived downstairs. With nostalgic empathy he says, "You always have the memories."

I was temporarily comforted. However, upon reflection, I also know that I am losing my memories. We all do. We thought we had memorized them. We become more grateful for the triggers: the old photos, the videos, the slideshows and vinyl records, the yellowed journals, and diaries. And the stories we retell to one another.

This is how we '-ize' something…take what just sits there, un-animated, and activate it once again. Actualize. Utilize. Galvanize. Memor-ize the lines and the moments by saying and telling, singing and playing aloud until they have a home in our hearts.

Since joining the elderly category, we forget easily, pause often in a recall mode, have a tough time remembering what day it is…none of which looks good on a resumé. Forgetful and unemployable, our significance seems to evaporate into the mist of bygone days.

But then an adult grandson phones. He tells us of his day-off plans and the details of his busy young life. Later, wishing we had memorized every line of dialogue and discussion, we try to think of every word he said, but our short-term memory fails us. However, our long-term memory shines through the blur as he activates times past. He remembers his grandpa's growing-up-on-a-farm stories about shoveling manure, filling silos, and milking those cows early and late. He tells us that now the empathy that grew out of listening has memory-muscled its way into his current work with exhausted farmers. He mentions his goal to read through the Bible in a year, then recalls us telling him years ago, when that was also a goal of ours, that having made it to Ezekiel we had to temporarily take leave of the Old Testament laments and leap into the hopeful messages of the New. Because of this, he chooses a reading plan with balance.

Oh, how we needed that phone call to revitalize our long-forgotten past! To realize that he had memorized (or immortalized) lines of our story by repeating them in his. Perhaps our significance 'stories' its way through successive generations…

After saying good-bye to our grandson, we heard this scenario repeated as we turned up the volume of our background music. The album featured pianist Rubenstein playing Chopin's composition of over a century ago: *Nocturne in F-flat sharp*. How many repetitions, how much memorizing and synthesizing has it taken to keep this music alive for nearly two hundred years? All echoes of Chopin's music would have faded had others not memory-stored those melodies and played them back to us. The sheet music of our lives stays silent unless…

Knowing we so easily forget, the God who authors stories re-played ours that day, moving our grandson to remember us and remember with us.

God knows us by heart. Memorized by the Divine, we are never forgotten.

Sketch and write your own lines

PARTY LINES

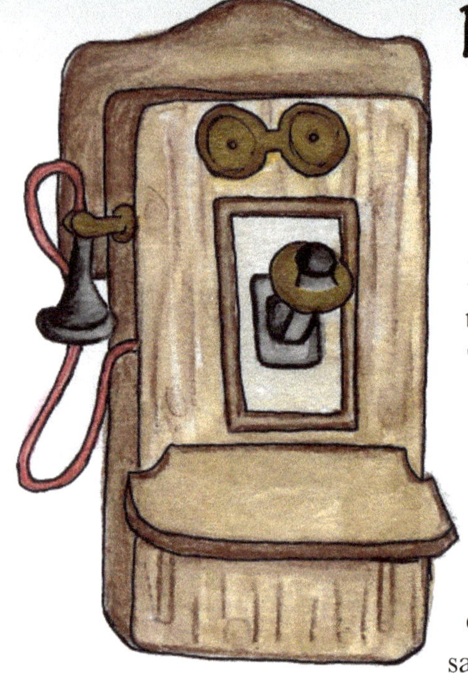

In the 1950's when our family visited relatives in rural Montana, I remember being intrigued by the large oak box that hung in the mudroom, just outside the kitchen door. There was a stool under it, a set-up that allowed the sitter to talk into a protruding black mouthpiece while holding a megaphone earpiece to an ear. Talking and listening. Through a telephone. Winding it up with a black handle on the right side summoned an operator who asked which 'party' you wanted to reach. Then she would plug you in, connecting you to your friend Susie Smith who was not in the same room, but miles down the road.

The tricky part had to do with privacy issues. Susie and my relatives were both on "party lines." Each of them shared their phone connections with eight or ten other farm families. They simply had different 'rings' assigned to them: two shorts and a long, three longs, one short and two longs, etcetera. You knew when "to pick up" because the phone call was clearly for you. But you also knew whose ring belonged to whom, and if you were curious, if you were prone to eavesdropping or gossip, you could quietly listen in without the other party knowing. The temptation to lose one's integrity and dishonor the privacy of another was daily, heralded by the ring of a bell and the promise of entertainment, all as close as your own kitchen door.

Nowadays our party lines have morphed into Facebook, Instagram, and TikTok where hundreds, even thousands, are privy to our information. We gladly post it, perhaps too gladly, not knowing who is "picking up" on our personal lives and how they interpret our motivations and identities.

I am writing these lines the day after a presidential election. We have been reeling for days, months even, under the bombardment of social media's input about party lines (those Democrat and Republican designations invented by our democratic republic). Each party line has its talkers and shouters. Truth is confused with lies; trust trampled. What has happened to these brilliant inventions for communicating, for helping humans understand one another? What has each of us contributed to corrupting the telephone and the iPhone with disruption and division, promoting exclusiveness and hatred? And when is it clearly none of our business?

Will we ever be able to extract ourselves from the party lines and simply come to the party?

The party where people laugh aloud at the balloons and glitter and fireworks. The party where all things fun and funny flourish. Where the guest list is from every tribe and nation. Where we sing and dance and applaud and shout praises; where we affirm others, listen to their stories when they choose to tell them, and love them with abandon.

A party with no dividing lines. That would be heaven on earth.

Sketch and write your own lines

PLUMBLINES

Guessing. Conjecture. I wonder what percentage of our thoughts are unsure. Offline in a wilderness cabin, I am without Googling benefits. And feeling a little 'off' about nearly everything without being able to 'look it up' or 'check it out.'

Without research, I can only question: Were plumblines invented before or after the wheel? When did structuring straightness become important? Maybe it was around 500 B.C when the Jewish people rebuilt their beloved Jerusalem from the rubble they found after a long exile. I am guessing Jewish boys learned to climb high on building projects and drop a long cord weighted by a rock to eyeball whether the stone walls of either home or temple lined up. A metaphor was born. The Torah, their book of laws, was called the 'plumbline' that kept their lives upright and holy, vertically aligned to their God.

And when did humanity begin to need levels? If plumblines adjusted all things vertically, certainly there was also need for measuring the horizontal, for achieving a smooth flatness that one could build upon. The cave men and women designed no floor plans or room arrangements, but the stone hut builders had to figure out a way to keep their walls from falling down. Then came the log cabin builders with their need to lay that first log 'on the level' lest the whole house go crooked and crumble too soon. A pioneer probably put a container of creek water on that first log and watched whether it brimmed evenly over the edges.

Now being replaced by digital measuring, plumblines used by building contractors for most of modern history still had long strings with a lead bob tied to the end, cone-shaped and very sharp at the point. The levels, long metal encasements with a see-though plastic tube, still used liquid with a bubble that centered itself between two black lines when placed on a perfectly flat surface.

If plumblines are a metaphor for getting-it-right with God vertically, then levels are those horizontal relationships with others. But hard as we work at using measuring gadgets (psychological assessments, spiritual disciplines, and mindfulness) to move us toward perfect bonds with God and with people, we miss the mark.

Consider Jesus plummeting from heaven into our human level, bursting the bubble of our attempts at perfection. Forgiven and free, our striving scatters. We let go of the all-consuming focus of plumblines and levels, exchanging straight and flat for surprises of joy and awe!

Jesus welcomes us into an abundant life far beyond the serious impossibilities of measuring tools and checklists. Instead of leaving His beloved ones in a constant self-struggle to become flawless, He invites us to enjoy His handmade beauties exploding like fireworks everywhere. Amazed by this display just for us, we experience wonders like the Aurora Borealis, ocean phosphorescence, a toddler laughing, the green flash at sunset over the Gulf, shooting meteors, families, rainbows gracing waterfalls, the blaze of sun on desert blooms, bonfires, the iridescence of hummingbird wings, births, autumn colors, lightning, and the radiance of a bride. All immeasurable bursts of light and love. Fireworks cannot be straightened by a plumbline or flattened by a level. But they do inspire awe and mark the beginning of countless celebrations.

Praise God from whom all blessings flow!

Sketch and write your own lines

POWER LINES

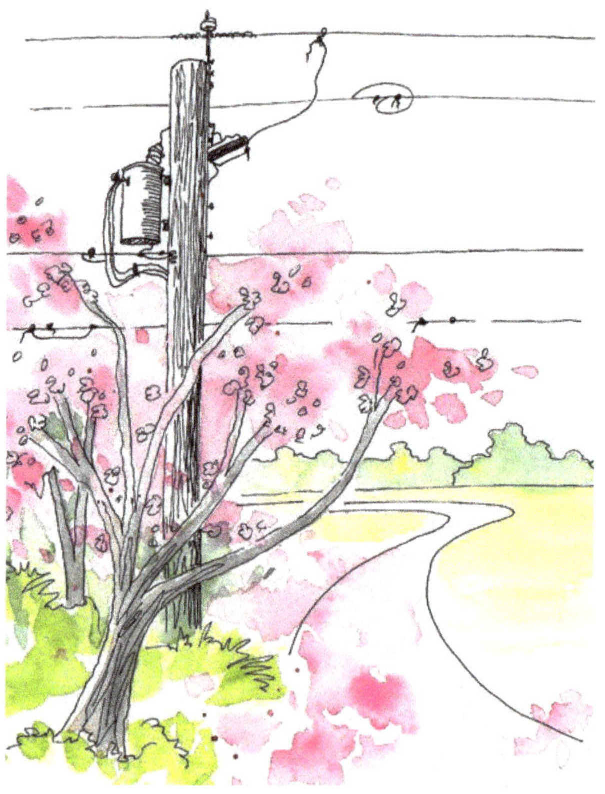

Mid-May the drifts swirl under power lines and across county roads. Pink snow from falling cherry blossoms covers curbsides and sidewalks. How much energy goes into generating this jaw-dropping beauty-blizzard? What life-power goes into pushing petals out of branches every single spring so they can let loose and change the ground to pink?

I drive to my May date at Starbucks, an entire franchise built on how coffee caffeinates and empowers conversation. We order our drinks and sit on high stools that let our feet dangle, hoping to get grounded once more in the middle of our highly mobilized lives. We have discussed these things before and often, she and I. "Should I go back to work now that my babies are one and three? What will it do to our family's equilibrium? Can I juggle it all? Can I still remember how to be a clinical psychologist?"

Many times, over the prior winter months, she has reported in about 'trying to make it happen': "Checked on office space and rent." "Researched licensing and re-instatement." "Put out feelers for childcare." "Discussed the pros and cons with my husband (endlessly, he would say)."

The puzzle pieces just would not, could not, fit-click into place.

But today she tells the rest of the story. "I was in this cooking group that makes frozen meals together, and standing in the kitchen next to me was a professional counselor I knew a long time back. She asks me how my practice is going. I admitted that it wasn't. Immediately, effortlessly, she invites me to join hers…and tosses in all the scheduling, aesthetic décor, reasonable rent, and professional support I would need."

I pick up on the word "effortlessly." "This seems to be the way God works," I respond. "We let up on our striving, and He plunks provision into our lives like blossoms falling, gently, with surprises of beauty. Slow-motion miracles of quiet, unseen life-power move us out of dormancy or depression or indecision."

We talked about power lines. How you do not see the electricity coursing through them, but oh, how they light up a world! Effortlessly.

Sketch and write your own lines

A ROOFLINE

I am on the cabin porch, my deckchair positioned precisely beneath the roofline's shadow so that my vision can catch the sun without being blinded by it.

Our lone pine tree is the only other shade in the front of our hundred-year-old log cabin. That is why we keep it. Although we have amputated several dead limbs, though a 4th of July firecracker spark lit one whole side on fire, and even though it has carried darkish bearded moss on its branches for decades, we cherish it. For under this tree, we place our lawn chairs during summer's heat and get to know one another again more deeply…or live in the world of others while we read. It was my dad's favorite last spot before he died.

Today, though, this evergreen has God-messages for me. A reminder that if I sit still long enough in one place, in one moment of time miracle-ized by a timeless God, with the eyes of my heart open, I will see what I have never seen before…and quite possibly never again.

The upper branches of this bruised and wounded tree, silhouetted by the blue of a Montana sky, look like a towering candelabra. The piercing sun dazzles the tree's top…and there, in the perfect arc of the sun's movement across the universe, I watch the rays catch the wings of a thousand no-see-ums flying directly above the end of each branch as if lighting it on fire. They are scintillating candle flames, letting off rogue insect sparks that always return to the brilliance.

And then, above, behind, and through these iridescent flames, streaks of more light move quickly and unexplainably. Wait and watch. Move your chair a little to adjust the roofline's shade so you can see what the sun is playing with…ahhh, spider webs floating in the air like phosphorescent eels, lit up, then switched off by the wavering sun to tease me with their disappearing act.

I have never seen this before: insects undulating and spiders weaving, collaborating to ignite dancing flames above a treetop candelabra. A crown of glory, for sure.

Under an ordinary roofline the mundane becomes the unexpected and the extraordinary. This breath-taking show-and-tell by God closely follows my morning prayers for seven grandsons and two granddaughters, twenty-somethings who are in hyper-decision-making modes about what to do with their wild and wonderful lives. I add a postscript: *May You light up their paths, Lord. Give them the heart-sight for the no-see-ums of Yourself, and Your Love, and the next beyond-expectation happening. Amen.*

SIDE-LINED

Side-lined. That feeling of being taken out of the game, of being benched on the bottom row of bleachers, assigned to the non-participation of only watching and perpetually waiting. While just sitting there, worthlessness sets in, for starters. And then the reasons for being sidelined: not good enough, made too many mistakes, don't have what it takes, no fun to be around, a liability rather than an asset. Followed by the questioning: Why am I here anyway? Who needs me? Does anyone notice when I'm missing? Does anyone care?

It is a testament to my parents' good loving that I did not feel left out until I was at least five years old. I remember being the first inside the 1942 Ford as we loaded up for a family outing. I chose the front seat, sitting alone in the middle, savoring a place of favoritism between my parents, anticipating their warmth even as sunshine's promises fell on me through the windshield. But then the shuffle began. I was asked to move to the backseat with my little brother while my baby sister took up space on my mother's lap. I was bumped from first class. In the ensuing long ride to wherever, I felt alone, dismissed, relegated to a back corner. I felt my first little-girl-sized stab of abandonment; it lingers still.

The fear of abandonment has been with us since God banished Adam and Eve from the garden of Eden because they did not measure up. Perfection in creation was gone; so was perfection in their relationship. From those moments on, closeness to God and to each other would have its abandonment issues. There would be no perfect game of life with everyone always taking part and everyone always winning.

These days technology has worsened that loneliness. In tech-speak we talk about a FOMO diagnosis. Fear of Missing Out. Oh, to be that person on Facebook who has gone to the Swiss Alps, learned to yodel, and actually sat in John Calvin's chair at St. Pierre Cathedral in Geneva. Have you seen that masterful dance on Instagram? Why haven't you done that? Check out YouTube for that 93-year-old woman who ran the marathon. Learn her exercise routines so that you, too, can run races at her age. Multiply each of these missed possibilities by the bombardment from billions of people and blogs…and our math registers *impossibility*, leaving us confused, out in the cold, side-lined, and abandoned.

I was a first grader when my first bout with FOMO kicked in. Every morning our teacher would ask us to raise our hands if we were going to eat in the cafeteria that day. I had never been to the cafeteria; I had never even seen the cafeteria. Every day at lunchtime, I walked the two blocks home, ate lunch, and walked back. What had I been missing that my other classmates were experiencing? Curiosity and latent jealousy-by-comparison took over one morning. I raised my hand. The teacher looked surprised. "Do your parents know you are staying for lunch?" she asked. "Yes," I lied.

My parents phoned the school in response to their missing child. When the school day was over, they explained to me the worry I had put them through. My mother led me into the saved-for-company parlor and sat me next to the overstuffed arm of the blue-deep sofa. She explained that it was important for me to ask Jesus to forgive my sin of lying. I think He did. I don't remember a thing about the cafeteria, the place I was fearful I might not ever experience, saddened by the notion that others were in on something forbidden to me. However, I do remember the grace extended to me by Jesus and my mother that day.

Today I read this quote written by Dr. Curt Thompson: "Hell is the mental state of the fear of abandonment that we occupy" when we fail to see and take in "the gaze of the One who, when we are lost, is always coming to find us."

God does not abandon us even as we are side-lined for our imperfection. He immediately found Adam and Eve outside the garden and provided for their needs…food, clothing, shelter, love, forgiveness. His presence is oceanic and oxygenic, everywhere like water and air. There is nowhere we can go to hide from Him.

Not even on a bench. Or in whatever out-of-bounds place our side-lining has taken us. We can whisk the questions around in our mixed-up brain and stir in the negativity of our worthlessness to agitate ourselves. Or we can simply sit still, relax, and call this side-lining a time and place of rest. Then wait for the Lord's whispered aside to us, His side-lined ones: *"You are beloved, and you belong."* He is fully aware of us; His gaze is upon us. We are not lost to Him or ever left out by Him.

He always joins us, on the bench or in the game.

Sketch and write your own lines ⟶

SPINAL COLUMNS

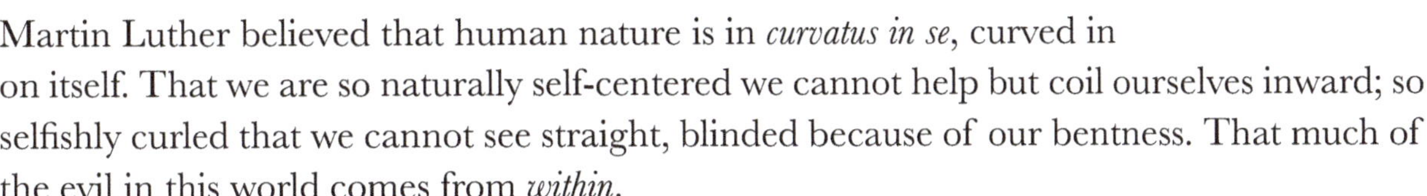

Perfect posture. A straight, perpendicular line from head to toe. Since our youth we have been admonished to sit up straight, walk tall, even balance a book on our heads for practice. But our default position is to fold in on ourselves, hunch over…a habitual curvature of the spine. Rather than strong vertical columns, we slump into slouches.

Dozens in my peer group go for massages and acupuncture treatments to alleviate stress and neck pain caused by inattention to remain upright. Might that be analogous to bending rules and putting stress on our moral fiber? At first do we stoop just a little… and then a little more, until we have scoliosis of our value systems? "And gradually, though no one remembers exactly how it happened, the unthinkable becomes tolerable. And then acceptable. And then legal. And then applaudable," says Joni Erickson Tada.

Martin Luther believed that human nature is in *curvatus in se*, curved in on itself. That we are so naturally self-centered we cannot help but coil ourselves inward; so selfishly curled that we cannot see straight, blinded because of our bentness. That much of the evil in this world comes from *within*.

Walking tall is tough to sustain. But the truth is, we are made to bear weight. We are a bunch of spinal columns moving through life. Lines that are solid, erect, perpendicular, and strong. Think Greek temples or colonial churches or the Lincoln memorial. Columns holding up buildings. We can become that temple not made with hands that God describes in the Bible: *"Don't you realize that all of you together are the temple of God and that the Spirit of God lives in you?" — I Corinthians 3:16 NLT* We are strategically placed columns holding up a communal building of faith. "She is the backbone of her family," we say. "He is the backbone of the community." "They are pillars of the church."

But do you, do I, have the spine to stabilize this kind of weight? Nope. First, as God's temple columns, we need individual and supernatural attention so that we no longer fall inward on ourselves, bent and broken. Sin within is removed and replaced by strength within. It's called forgiveness, a love-gift from Jesus. Once forgiven, any one of us can walk tall.

We stand or walk aright when our head and heart are postured in perfect alignment. Spinal columns do that. When one's heart says you *are beloved*, imagine that knowledge moving up the spinal cord to a brain that answers *I believe that*. God's Spirit sends messages back and forth through 18 inches of vertical vertebrae to help us know we are His forgiven favorites. He lines up our heartfelt compassions with our rational values so that we can, with more assurance, walk and stand alongside others and sometimes even carry them.

Carrying others while still walking tall? Yep. Do-able because of the God who made spinal columns, completely forgives, and dwells in human temples. Sounds like the perfect posture to me.

Sketch and write your own lines

SOCIAL DISTANCING

Go ahead. Draw a line between two people, maybe between a grandmother and a grandchild. Wedge it like a knife slicing through their embrace. Split their hug down the middle. Next, require that they back away from one another at least three steps each. Then demand, with elements of fear and shame, that they stay six feet apart for the coming days and weeks and months. Add face masks to hide their smiles and muffle their conversations. Tell them to go to their separate homes, stay there, and be safe. Pretend that screen time can be fully as relational as the bodily warmth of togetherness. Zoom with talking heads instead of engaging in conversations between fully present people. Choose the hard metal and plastic devices over the soft and vibrant body language that fades if not renewed. Trade embraces for emptiness.

Social distancing is an oxymoron. Being social is a coming together; distancing is moving apart. This line of separation "they" are drawing between us? Inherent in every inch of that dividing line is impossibility. No one can surgerize relationships. They are indivisible and overlapping. An embrace takes two people. So does eye contact and soulmate bonding. Closeness and intimacy are basic human needs on the health-and-quality-of-life continuum. I am in your story; you are in mine. Even God makes the restoring of relationship a supernatural priority.

How ironic that to protect the health of the 'vulnerable, at-risk elderly,' people are told to stay away from them, help them isolate, sanitize everything and everybody against the Covid19 virus of 2020. We learned a new vocabulary to keep us in line: do social distancing, shelter in place, stay home, stay safe, quarantine, PPE (personal protective equipment), face masks, ventilators, vaccines, testing for antibodies. We had suggestions for creatively 'staying in touch' while not touching: wave through windows, talk through devices, show your face on a screen. But don't go near anyone.

So, the whole world goes into lockdown and stays away from each other. And just exactly how do we obey the nourishing necessities of "one-anothering?" Like bearing one another's burdens. Or devoting ourselves to one another. Respect, get along, love, encourage, live in harmony, accept, forgive, teach, and comfort one another. From a distance? Six feet or more apart? Forever?

As one of the at-risk elderly, I am putting this in writing. This social distancing line between us? This maddening separation done out of love to protect me and keep me safe? Just sayin': it is not natural or healthy. And if it is not temporary, I am asking all my children and grandchildren to break the rules and cross that line. Be bold and radical because your mother is giving you permission and your grandmother has asked you to. Come and give me a hug.

Sketch and write your own lines

SILHOUETTE LINES

It was 1948 when teachers shared the latest popular, contagious craft: making silhouettes of each pupil to give to their parents as Christmas gifts. The set up was monumental: Place an 18" high stage beneath the blackboard, set a small wooden chair sideways on said stage, acquire a very bright light just the right height, and tape a large sheet of white art paper to the blackboard. Ask the small child to sit very still for a long time as the light 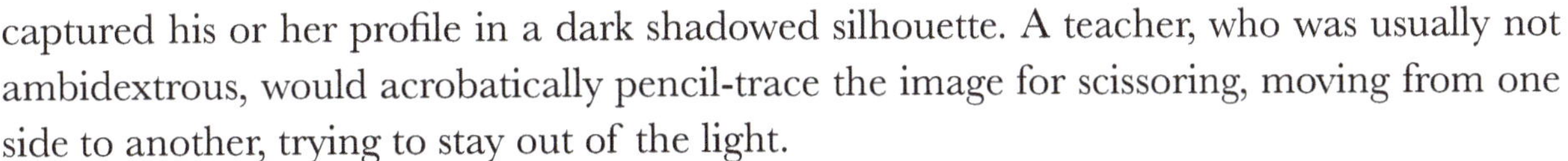 captured his or her profile in a dark shadowed silhouette. A teacher, who was usually not ambidextrous, would acrobatically pencil-trace the image for scissoring, moving from one side to another, trying to stay out of the light.

I can still hear two teachers discussing what to do with me. Because of my long bundle of blonde hair, my profile looked like a small haystack with a nose-shaped bump coming out of the side. "How do we give her a neck?" they sighed. One of them decided to lift my hair while the other outlined not only my neck but chopped off my long hair with some deft drawing so that my "whole" profile could fit on the paper. And should they leave the horn-shaped hump of my hair-ribbon? Later, when I saw my own black silhouette glued to a white background, my little girl thought was: *That isn't the real me.*

Silhouettes are popular because we like simplicity, the stark and plain lines that give us instant recognition without too much wondering. *It is what it is*, we say.

Granted, the blackened shapes of trees against a setting sun quiet me as my senses wind down. When there is less to take in or process, a focused beauty does filter through. Everywhere there is a clear silhouette line, dimmer light is always present. Brighter light showcases more than just outlines. The stimulants add up: a three-dimensional world full of color and shading, the complexities of matter and space, and the intermingling of it all.

I am charmed by the logo our grown son engineered to market their Dancing for Joy studio. It messages easily from coffee mugs and sweatshirts, building marquees and posters. But it doesn't give the whole picture. Its simple outline was digitally extracted from a photo of his wife dancing on a beach in Hawaii—a real person, not just an image…full of zest and story, creativity and agility, risk, and joy. Those delightful aspects of one God-created individual take a lifetime to live into and cannot be captured in a few clean silhouette lines.

During the Lenten season we will focus again on the most familiar silhouettes of all time: three crosses on a hill. We think there is clarity in outlines and monochromatic black—but there is so much more to the cross story than that. There's a real live person involved. His name is Jesus. He declares *I am the Resurrection and the Life*, then dies for us, eradicating evil's darkness, and conquering death. He embodies life itself in all its mystery and invites us to embrace all that is life-giving and whole along with Him.

When we try to depict any living thing with the simple lines of a silhouette, we are de-picturing reality into a flatness without a second or third dimension…perhaps even leaving out a fourth or fifth. Francis of Assisi wrote: *The visible world is an active doorway to the invisible world, and the invisible world is much larger than the visible.* Enjoy the simplicity of silhouette lines but do remember this: There is more; there is always more.

Sketch and write your own lines

STANDING IN LINE

We would rather not. Standing in line seems such a waste. We try to predict and time how to avoid the rush at the box office, the line at the check-out, traffic jams, customs lines at borders, boarding ships and planes, and getting a driver's license or a flu shot or a table at a favorite restaurant. We are stuck…and being stuck causes frustration, impatience, and sometimes even anger. We could blame our consumer culture and American government for those lines, the ones required to stand in that put us at a standstill. No matter that the person-shaped bodies taking up space in those lines are us…which makes us part of the problem.

We even dare to hope there will be no line, no other people who also eat and buy groceries, get immunized or travel, need help with their paperwork, or attend performances or ballgames. If our hope is realized and there is no line, we worry, then wonder if we are in the right place on the right day or whether we missed the cancellation notice, or if some kind of apocryphal event has happened to wipe out humanity. And, paradoxically, we feel alone.

There are lines I would gladly stand in because of the reward waiting at the front of the line. How long, I wonder, would I stand in line to experience a hug from a grandchild? Or to secretly observe my husband's compassion as he cares for patients in a wound clinic? How long could I wait to meet a friend I had not seen for forty years? To be with an estranged brother? To be in on a breakthrough for mental illness? To see peace flourish between nations? To have every tear wiped away?

Sometimes we expect to stand in line, but then we don't have to. My husband and I imagined waiting forever, along with impossible circumstances, to catch Eugene Peterson in a book signing of his translation and paraphrase of the entire Bible into contemporary language. Later, by Montana wagon train standards, we became neighbors a few hours apart during summer vacations. So there he was, with his wife Jan, sharing chips and dip with us in our living room telling stories about the calling and challenges of producing *The Message*. This is a book to stand in line for…for a very long time. Read silently or aloud, the meanings and truths of the Bible move into instant understanding. No waiting and muddling. The words, because they are already ours, hit home. Here is a sample:

*He [God] decided from the outset to shape the lives of those who love Him along the same lines as the life of his Son. The Son **stands first in the line** of humanity he restored. We see the original and intended shape of our lives there in Him.* — Romans 8:29

We are all standing in line, really…waiting for our lives to turn out. When there is someone outstanding at the head of the line, someone like God's son Jesus, to follow, to imitate, to believe in, our waiting is energized with purpose. Our patience changes from passive to passionate. While we are in line, we are becoming unstuck and shaped into a longed-for wholeness. We are being made fully alive by a perfectly capable God and a bunch of imperfect people standing with us who like the idea of becoming like Jesus. And we are not alone.

Come…stand in this line…over here with us. It's moving….

Sketch and write your own lines

TIMELINES

She said we think time is in a line. Then she picked up the end of a string with one forefinger and thumb, moved her other forefinger and thumb across the string, making it taut, showing that the string came to an end. "And time is not really like that," she told the children sitting in a circle at her feet. She then tied the two ends of the string together and shaped it into an undisputed roundness. "There is no end to time," she said as her finger traced the circle again and again.

Timelines are about history and schedules. Circles are about infinity.

Jesus entered earth's timeline, picked each of us up and tied all our knots into an infinity of unexplainable duration: eternal life for each of us. One of my grandsons explained this to me when he was little…about six years old on his timeline. His innocent wisdom defies logic, reminding me of how Jesus explained himself while He was on earth:

Revelation 22:13 I'm A to Z, the First and the Final, Beginning and Conclusion. Jesus.

Following is the story of little Caleb's conclusions:

We designate Saturday to help with the renovation of a 1920's fixer upper. Our daughter and her husband have purchased an old house with redemption thoughts in mind. Not wanting to leave us out of the adventure, they have included us in the remodeling job descriptions. Grandpa, dressing the part, looks like Bob the Builder with his plaid shirt and tool belt. Grandma is ready to sacrifice watching Yellow School Bus videos with grandchildren and wield a paintbrush instead.

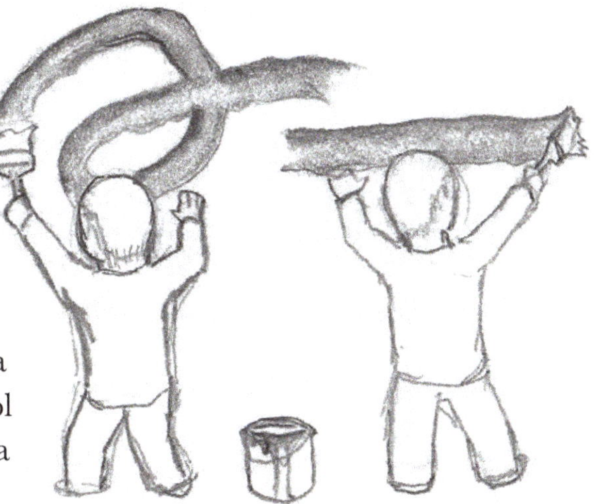

The grandsons opt to help Grandma paint. Anthony, our eldest at age eight, uses a tack cloth to wipe off every speck of dust from an old door balanced on two sawhorses. His moves are deliberate and patient. Younger brother Caleb, on the other hand, dips his brush into the paint can before the contents are stirred and swoops the heavy drips eagerly toward the waiting door. I try to give "finishing touches" a new meaning before the paint dries into mooshy mounds rather than flat surfaces. We talk about our teamwork and how good it will all look when we are done and why Mom wants all the woodwork painted white.

Caleb pouts a little. "I wonder why she didn't choose yellow for any of the rooms."

I have the cheerful comeback: "Just wait until you grow up, Caleb. Then you can buy a house of your own and paint it any color you choose."

"Not if your wife doesn't want it that color," his older brother knowingly chimes in.

"What would you do, if your wife wanted blue and you wanted yellow?" I ask.

Anthony answers while Caleb voices agreement, "I'd argue with her about it until I won, just like I do with Caleb." I grin, silently thinking that, even though brother-to-brother negotiating is good practice, these little boys will learn much about the merits of marital compromise someday.

"Why do you always pick yellow, Caleb?" I ask.

"Because 'Y' is only two away from 'A'," he explains, making very little sense.

"What do you mean, Caleb?" I pursue.

"Like, instead of A, B, C, you go the other way. A…Z…Y. See?" He says each letter slowly, hoping his grandma will grasp the full meaning of doing the alphabet backwards, even when you start with A. I begin mentally moving my linear alphabet into a circular one, like Caleb's. "Z comes next to Y…only two away from A," he explains. Then he states his final reasoning: "And yellow begins with Y."

He looks at me over the smears of wet paint hoping I get the picture: he wants a favorite color that is centered, close to the beginning and close to the end, a yellow flag waving in the circle of infinity. His undeniable truth remains: timelines are circular after all.

I hope his wife understands.

Prayer: *Timeless Jesus, our understanding of you is small and incomplete. As is life. And timelines. You are the Alpha and Omega, the A to Z, the beginning and the end. You encompass every letter of every alphabet. Help us to find our center in the Y word: You. Amen.*

Sketch and write your own lines ⟶

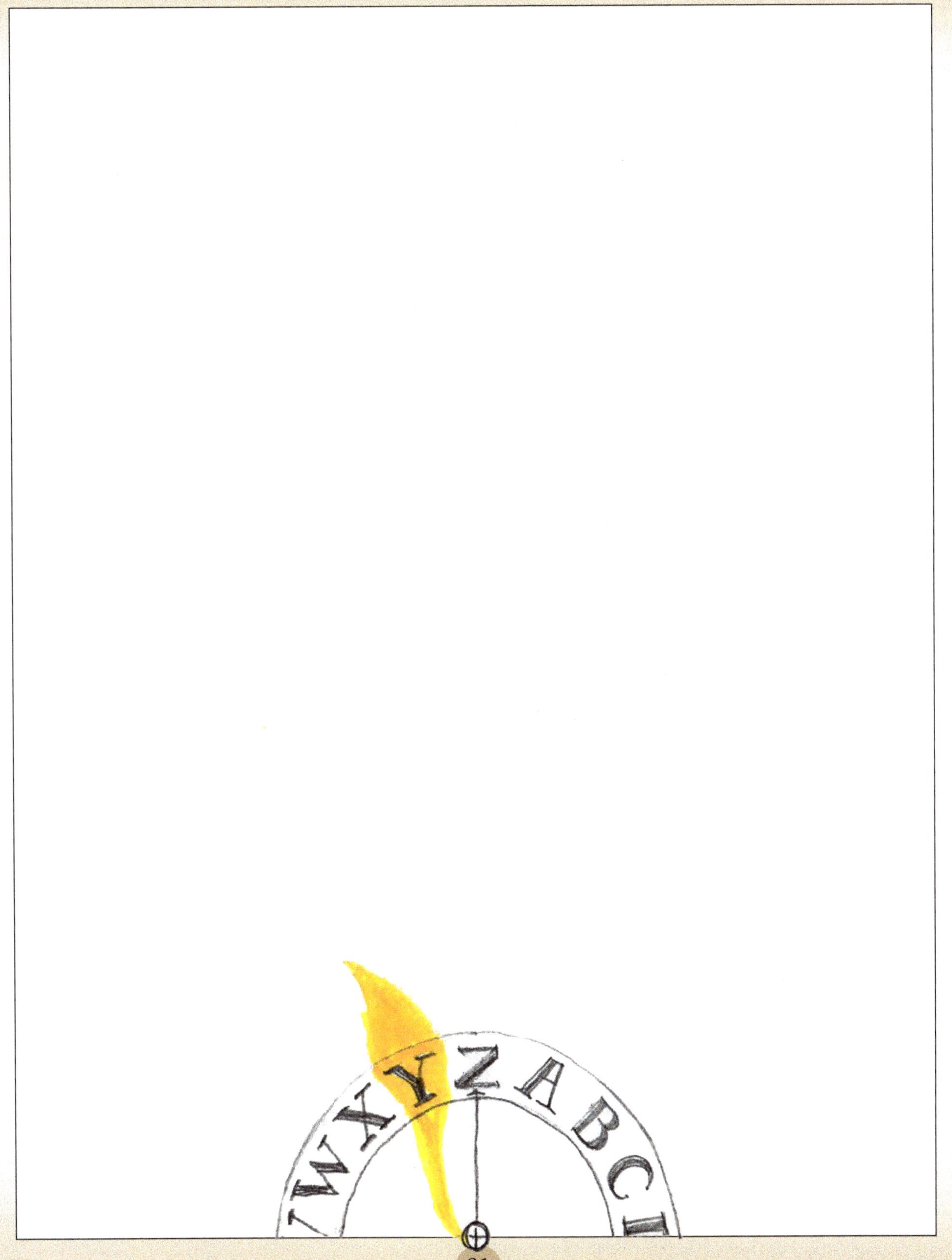

WRINKLE LINES

"Tell all the truth but tell it slant—" writes the poet Emily Dickinson. How does that apply to facing my face full-on in the mirror each morning? These wrinkles are my very own, sketched into the parchment of my skin, illustrations of every story I have lived and lived through. The truth about all these slanty, zigzagged lines is that they are not going away. Some furrows are deep enough to gather dust if I don't keep moving. William Shakespeare gave good advice about how to keep those facial lines on the move when he wrote "with mirth and laughter let old wrinkles ooze…" Better that than the acne of adolescence.

I like Madeleine L'Engle's novel title *A Wrinkle in Time*. Her fiction is my reality. My sense of time folds in on itself as if the calendar pages are creased into paper fans and Tuesday disappears between Monday and Wednesday. Or another fold wrinkles July into June before June is over.

My aging brain has thought-wrinkles, a delightful, somewhat delusional way of reframing facts into positive perspectives. For instance, as I face my aging future, looms come to mind, as in "The gathering gray *looms* on the horizon." A threatening storm-spiral of doom and decay. Surprises of dismay rather than delight. I can look forward to less mobility with more pain physically. Oh, and less mental agility with more forgetfulness.

A thought-wrinkle can reframe that "sense of loom" as well. Instead of a dismal future, imagine a creative weaving process. Looms are a fabulous invention for making both fabric and a familiar metaphor. An anonymous writer described each of us as a unique and colorful tapestry. But my human tendency is to view that piece of woven art from the underside, displaying it backwards on the wall of my life so that I see the wrinkles and loose threads, the tangles and knots—a kind of unexplained ugliness with no theme.

But sitting at the loom of my life, the masterpiece Maker throws the shuttle through well-placed strands, watches from a front and center position and enjoys the progress toward a preplanned, perfect finish. Just as there is a point on the shuttle in every loom directing each thread into place, keeping the back-and-forth in line, the entire process working into a purposeful pattern, so there is a point to aging. The design of my life continues developing to the very outer edges, until the Artist deems it "well done."

Instead of mirror-gazing that highlights my wrinkle lines, I shall forget the mirror and still remember who I am and who I have been. Furthermore, as a good exercise in down-sizing, I may just chuck the mirror. And then rehang the tapestry, frontside out. It's a keeper.

Sketch and write your own lines

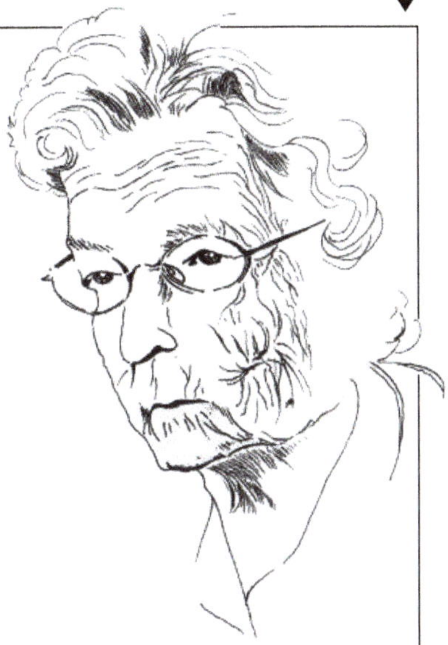

↓

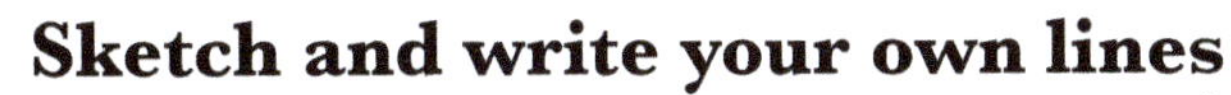

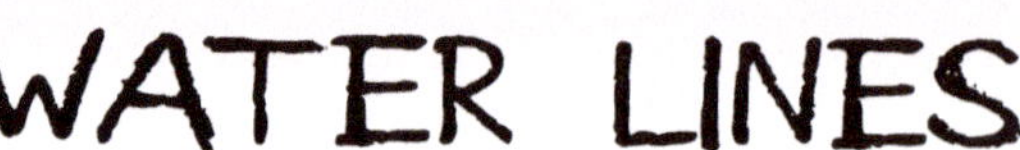 WATER LINES

Water lines are usually about water levels. Like that line still visible on the side of the house where the flood of '97 left its mark. But let me begin even more literally…with lines about water.

When the waiter at the Italian restaurant finds me waiting, he repeats his scripted opening line.

"Can I bring you sparkling or still water while you settle in?" Those possibilities were new to these old ears. In 'my day' water was served from a faucet, not in bottled or filtered or infused form. These choices felt like pure liquid luxury: still or sparkling.

Sparkling water triggers a quote from Ann Lamott: "Laughter is carbonated holiness." What lovely choices these: still water or sparkling. Today, sitting at this restaurant table, I choose sparkling.

Still water revives memories of sitting in an Adirondack chair on the porch deck of our wilderness cabin overlooking our tiny lake. Sometimes the water was so unmoving that the mirrored reflections of surrounding trees and mountains could be mistaken for the real thing. Awe filled me often in that place. I resonated with the poet of Psalm 23: *He leads me beside still waters.* Solitude and reflection are necessary things for a soul. A holy listening. Sometimes, under cover of the porch's overhang, I watched a torrential downpour 'ruin' the water's smooth surface. I laughed out loud (holy laughter?) as the surprise drama pulled me from sitting still, into a dance under the wild pelting of wet rain. What a quick-change artist God is! Ahhh…. And then the rainbow…

Yesterday I wrote a few lines about water levels in a graduation letter to a grandson:

Dear Josiah,

I recently found snippets of notes about you when you were about three years old. Our family had gone to the Oregon coast in the middle of May. When we found the beach made ever so expansive by a low tide, you didn't walk or run. You danced. Your hips had puppet strings pulled upward by an angel to make your feet kick. "Fancy feet," you dubbed them. You dance-stretched your open arms to the east and west, the north and south, with an all-encompassing embrace of creation's freedom.

You reminded me of the 'running scene' in <u>Chariots of Fire</u>, also on a beach, in which the protagonist proclaims, "God takes pleasure in me when I run." You take your shoes off and twirl, stand on your hands, zigzag, follow seagulls, run into our arms for hugs, then return to your moves…and God takes pleasure in you when you dance.

At one point you determine that all of grandpa's footprints should be smoothed out. You hunch down, and one by one, give them a tiny sandblast from your toddler hands, fingerpainting the wet sand back into place. We decided someday to ask you, "Why?"

When you noticed this grandma walking alone, you took my hand. For months I had been overwhelmingly busy. Time was like a waterslide, gushing, and swirling in a speed-chute since the countdown on New Year's Eve. The fear of feeling frantic had been roaring in my ears until now. I could hardly breathe.

But you stopped time for me, Josiah. The ocean waves did not roar; they quieted my soul. You taught me that you cannot dance on a waterslide. A beach at low tide is the better choice.

Water lines; water levels. Glasses half full or half empty. Often thirsting; sometimes drowning.

Jesus calls himself *living water*. I'll order a glass of that for a life-full of drinking Him in.

Sketch and write your own lines

AIRLINES

Our vacation is over. We reflect on the "unpredictables" of travel, the unplanned anecdotes, the mysterious reasons for our journey. Was it getting to know a friend's new husband or was it my husband's doctoring skills used to save a diabetic's foot? Maybe it was the connection to our former condo owners, the processing of a dear friend's grief, the soul-filling walks on the beach, the reunion with a grandson, or simply the gift of sunshine. Or was it sitting next to Jesus on the flight home?

We board the Tampa-Seattle plane and wonder who our seat partner will be. He is by the window engrossed in an audio book. The two of us settle…look at each other and agree, "He looks like Jesus might have." I am next to him wondering how one might begin a conversation with Jesus. The flight is half over when he takes out his earphones and orders coffee with sugar. I bravely ask him: "Seattle. Are you going home?" "No," he says. "On to Oregon."

"And what were you doing in Florida?"

"A eulogy for my grandmother's funeral." *Wow*! I think to myself. *Of course, a grandmother would want Jesus to do her eulogy!*

His lineage is Brazilian and South African. His father died when he was three. His mother left him in the care of a grandmother when he was six. He was moved around to boarding schools and "safe" places most of his young life to avoid the threatening dangers of apartheid. Parochial schools introduced him to Christianity. Division and violence and always-on-the-move characterized his life. *A Biblical phrase comes to me: Nowhere to lay his head.*

Finally making it to the U.S., he got an education in the arts and sculpturing and then taught at the university level. He shared that being a professor to millennials was difficult because every student was an art critic, but none would accept helpful criticism. He decided to find something else. Taken by the American history of settlement and intrigued by Lewis and Clark, he loaded his car and drove west. Which is how he got to Oregon.

Before that, however, he managed to travel the world, and simply pick up and go places… honoring his restlessness. He helped with tsunami repair in Thailand for two years, living with various families who were Buddhist, Hindu, and Muslim. He discovered how helpless he was in the face of such mass destruction and upheaval in people's lives. His humanity and his humility are palpable.

The conversation turns delightful and deep. "Chaos and harmony go hand in hand," he says. "Like microscopic red and white blood cells that are warring all the time in our bodies…but if we should choose one over the other, we would die. Life is about both/and rather than either/or. It's all about magnification," he says. "Standing back and seeing the wider picture." *Through the eyes and mind of God,* methinks. His brown eyes are piercing. "And forgiveness…forgiveness is major." *Sounds exactly like something Jesus would say.*

"What about you?" he asks, exuding care about me. An otherness focus oozes out of him. I explain how I was born into a Christian family, embraced those beliefs, and eventually attended a denominational college.

"What college?" he asks. When I respond, he says, "Oh, I have friends from there!"

Of course, you do, I think to myself. *Doesn't Jesus have a knack for knowing everyone everywhere?*

The dialogue continues. He makes me feel like even *my* brain and heart can play with philosophy and theology, closing the meaning gap between thinking and feeling. I ask more questions, not wanting this conversation to stop. We talk about suffering next.

"Think of a kaleidoscope," he encourages. "All those broken pieces, when viewed through the eyepiece, become a beautiful piece of art. Do you know what kaleidoscope means in Greek?" Then he explains the syllables: *kali* - beautiful, *eddo* - form, *scope* - look. "Imagine standing back and seeing beauty in each person instead of brokenness, then pulling away further and feeling awe at how many of them there are, the billions and the history, suspending yourself in space and viewing the blue pearl we call earth, and beyond that the wonder of the whole universe. "Magnification," he reiterates. *And mystery*, I think and then dare say aloud.

Together we agree that God, indeed, exists. I share about how matter and meaning, mystery and metaphor sometimes move me to write. As do my grandkids who surprisingly gave me God-messages. "Out of the mouths of babes," he says, quoting Jesus. "Yes," I say…and explain that is exactly why I titled the book *Out of the Mouths of Grandbabes*. We exchange information when he decides his mother would like that book.

He sculpts things. Calls himself a blacksmith who is trying to keep alive a lost art. Creates massive, heavy, rustic art from bronze and iron for stadiums, banks, and mansions. He works out of a forge in a small town in Oregon.

"Why there?" I ask.

"A girl," he says. "I followed her to her hometown. We are obsessed with each other, I guess. It's the first time I have felt loved."

"Will you marry her?" I asked.

"I am afraid to ask. Not settled enough. I don't know what family is like except for fights about finances. And divorce." A sadness comes over him. "My mother just told me at the funeral that she wants a divorce from my stepfather."

"I'm so sorry," I say. After a long pause, I bravely ask, "How old are you?"

"Thirty-three."

I pause again, remembering that Jesus was exactly that age when he died on the cross for us and resurrected, finished with His work on earth.

"Has anyone ever told you that you look like Jesus?" I ask.

"Yes," he answers smiling. "Not a bad look, would you say?"

"Not a bad look at all," I agree. "And now I know that Jesus takes two sugars in His coffee."

"And two creams," he adds.

The Bible speaks to all our unsettled hearts about how people keep faith: *"They…accepted the fact that they were transients in this world. People who live this way make it plain that they are looking for their true home. If they were homesick for the old country, they could have gone back any time they wanted. But they were after a far better country than that—heaven country. You can see why God is so proud of them, and has a City waiting for them. — Hebrews 11:14-16*

Sketch and write your own lines ⟶

THE LAST LINE

There isn't one.

GRATITUDE AND ACKNOWLEDGEMENTS

In its early planning stages, this book felt like a wedding without groomsmen and bridesmaids. Thank you to the beautiful humans who enhanced *LINES* with color and personality through their sketches:

Amy Brandt – young friend of the author (pages 26, 51, 70, 94)
Gini Bunnell – old new friend of the author (pages 4, 28, 41, 85)
Caleb Maiocco – 3rd grandson of the author (pages 64, 81, 89, 91)
Jack Vander Griend – 4th grandson of the author (pages 11, 16, 31, 33)
Josiah Vander Griend – 6th grandson of the author (page 13)
Donna Vander Griend – author (page 77)
Karen VerBurg – longtime friend of the author (pages 1, 2, 74, 87, 93)

Weddings and books do better with approval and attendees. Thank you, my supportive sisters, for proofreading *LINES* toward its publishing finish.

Laurie Arndorfer
Cheryl Bostrom
Michelle Holladay
Tammy LaPlante
Vicki Veltkamp Larson